Ó SÉ

A Kerry Family

—

A Football Dynasty

MARC Ó SÉ

WITH ADRIAN RUSSELL

GILL BOOKS

Gill Books
Hume Avenue
Park West
Dublin 12
www.gillbooks.ie

Gill Books is an imprint of M.H. Gill and Co.

9781804582237

Design origination by Typo•glyphix
Edited by Heidi Houlihan
Proofread by Sally Vince
Printed and bound in the UK using 100% renewable electricity at CPI Group (UK) Ltd
This book is typeset in Minion Pro by Palimpsest Book Production Limited, Falkirk, Stirlingshire

The paper used in this book comes from the wood pulp of sustainably managed forests.

A CIP catalogue record for this book is available from the British Library.

5 4 3 2 1

FSC www.fsc.org
MIX
Paper | Supporting responsible forestry
FSC® C013604

I have been blessed with fierce women and strong men.

For my wife Ellen, my rock and love of my life.
To our blessings, Alice, Tadhg and Tommy.

For my mother, Joan, a tireless worker in the family home at Ard an Bhóthair.

And to three great men …

Dad, Páidí and Tom

CONTENTS

PREFACE

Ar scáth a chéile a mhaireann na daoine.
(It's in each other's shadow that people live.)

To walk into Páidí Ó Sé's pub is to open a scrapbook. The inside is wallpapered with memories – photos of my uncle Páidí winning cups and holding them with his friends, legends of the game. Pictures of taoisigh, music icons, Hollywood stars, all taken under this roof. Old rivals, the local people who were there through it all, our An Ghaeltacht teams who took on the rest of Kerry first and then the country. Some scrapbook.

To me, it's a family album too. I grew up running the bases from our happy homeplace across the crossroads, to our grandmother's shop a few doors up, to this pub, which has always been so full of life. Great memories with my parents, uncles and three brothers who blazed a trail before me. It's here I served behind the counter, exchanging porter for tales of Kerry's long-gone footballers, and tried to keep up with traditional music maestros on the accordion my father bought me.

But I can see the spot too at the end of the bar where an All-Ireland winner innocently said, 'I heard the Ó Sés are rearing three footballers and a musician.' It was a throw-away joke but it needled a youngster who was full of doubt. Would I ever be good enough to play for Kerry? Was I the one who would break the chain? Would I fail to make it out of this family's long shadow?

Perhaps people think my surname brought privilege and benefits and, of course, that's true. But there was a price to be paid too. Like my uncles and brothers, there are now photographs of me inside the pub wearing green and gold. Páidí ran out in that jersey with the senior team for the first time in 1974; I finished up in 2016.

One can sketch out the modern history of the GAA in the span of those seasons. Our family tree stretches back before that though …

CHAPTER 1

LÁ LE CAITLIN

The story starts in west Kerry but takes a detour to the pavements grey of London, the 'city of fog and strange consonants', as Eavan Boland put it.

Our family is strongly associated with a piece of real estate at Ard an Bhóthair – with the wild Atlantic on one side and Sliabh an Iolair, Mount Eagle, on the other. It's beautiful and has always attracted people from around the country and beyond for holidays.

But emigration is part of the landscape too. My grandfather Tommy Ó Sé was a teenager when he left west Kerry in the 1930s, seeking to find employment and build a life for himself. Like many others he chose London, where there was a network of old neighbours and Irish contacts. He settled well and worked hard.

One of 15 children, Beatrice Lavin – my grandmother – arrived in the same destination, having left Ballymoate in Co. Sligo in 1935 at the age of 16.

Beatrice and Tommy met and became a couple. They married in 1938 and, it's evident even now, were a great team – working various jobs and trying to carve out a life for themselves. At one point, Beatrice rose each morning in the early hours to take on a milk round before going to her full-time job in a local hospital. The couple eventually ran a boarding house together – though Tommy still worked outside the home too. My grandmother was a really hard worker, all through her life. We wonder did that gene skip a couple of generations.

She worked ferociously hard and brought in good money from that B&B business, which they built up. It was a foreshadowing of their lives. Beatrice gave birth to two sons, Michael – my father – and my uncle Tom, and they were a happy family unit.

I remember my dad telling a story that my grandfather Tommy was making his way home through London one evening on his bicycle when he was knocked down by a lorry. It was a serious incident and he was in a lot of bother. I have a lovely letter at home that my father wrote to his dad while in hospital over the Christmas period. My father is around five or six years old and he's saying, 'I hope you'll be home for Christmas, Daddy,' and 'We miss you.' It makes me emotional, thinking of my dad as a young boy in a big city like London writing a letter like that, and how his father must have felt away from his family. I can put myself in that position now.

My grandfather was in and out of hospital a lot afterwards. It affected his life afterwards and I'm not sure if he ever recovered from that belt of a lorry on the cobbled streets of London. Prompted by the accident, he wanted to return to Ventry and the couple made plans to uproot their little family.

Tommy had received compensation after the incident, they had some of their own saved money and I'd imagine Tommy's family back in Kerry helped.

In 1955, they invested in a small shop at the crossroads of Ard an Bhóthair – maybe a mile from Ventry. They arrived off the bus at the crossroads on the feast day of St Caitlin, the patron saint of Ventry – 25 November. It has always been a special day in the parish.

It was fitting they arrived on this particular day. Their return meant we would all be born and reared in this hallowed part of the south-west of Ireland on the edge of the Atlantic.

The same year, Beatrice gave birth to their third son in Tralee General Hospital: Páidí. That would tell you my father was around thirteen and a half years older than Páidí. They reckon Páidí was a surprise. He certainly proved to be some surprise.

The family established themselves quickly at Ard an Bhóthair. Beatrice turned that shop into a busy hub of the community, a place where you could buy bread or you could buy a brush. You could buy paint. You could buy meat. You could buy whatever you wanted inside in that shop. It was just one of those shops where you could go and get anything.

And they were lucky too – or maybe clever – in that the creamery was back the road just 200 yards and all the farmers would come into the shop after delivering there and do all their shopping. That's where the Ó Sés properly started out.

It's funny now to think of my father, Michael, at the age of 13, wandering around west Kerry in the 1950s with a Cockney accent. He got rid of it quick enough inside in the Sem – St Brendan's in Killarney, the famous football nursery. His brother Tom refused to go to boarding school, however, and instead went to Dingle CBS. They say he was driving to school in the days when even the teachers didn't have cars – he'd pass them on the road with a salute as they cycled in. He was a man before his time and knew how to make a few bob.

A teacher of mine, Pat Nelligan, would often tell me that Tom was a really classy footballer and obviously a proud man. He'd jokingly brag to us that he was the only Ó Sé who had an All-Ireland minor medal.

He was part of the 1963 Kerry team that beat Westmeath in Croke Park and he went on to become an U21 player. I suspect that, ultimately, he wasn't as fixated on progressing as some of the rest of us, and he didn't play senior. He was too rounded. When Tom died recently, his wife Rosanna gifted me his minor medal, which I cherish.

My mother was Joan Kavanagh, or as it was pronounced around here Joan 'Key-vane'. Her people were from Lispole originally, back in the road from Dingle, but being farming people they were relocated to different parts of the place over time.

The Land Commission gave my grandfather a farm in the Dingle parish – Baile Riach, just outside the town on the Ventry side. It was a good farm and location to get. The family story goes that it came about because of a political connection. My auntie Eileen in Dublin was married to Joe Cruise, who was a driver for de Valera.

My maternal grandmother sadly died young, on her way home from a pilgrimage to Lourdes, ironically. My mother, the eldest, was put in charge of the rest of the children, as was often the case in those types of circumstances at the time.

My mother and father met at around 17 or 18 years of age and were courting for a while as young people.

But emigration turned a twist in the tale again. My mother, Joan, qualified as a nurse and moved to England and made her own way in the world. She worked hard taking care of people in busy hospitals for a few years.

The romantic story that we were told around the kitchen table was that our father got a notion, or worked up the courage, to go over to London one weekend. There, he swept her off her feet one fateful Saturday and brought her home.

I don't know if it panned out that way but that was my dad's version. It's nice to think there's some truth to it. I'm glad he made the ferry in time and made a convincing case once he got to London or things might have worked out different for a few of us.

Back home my father was playing his bit of football – he lined out for the Kerry junior side – but he wasn't too seriously into it. We often ball hopped that he was a sunshine player.

The elder two siblings though certainly weren't as serious about the football as the baby brother Páidí would go on to be. But not many were.

My mom was one of five. There was Paddy, Eily, Mickey and Mary too, but it's only Mary and my mom who are still alive. The others suffered throughout their lives from kidney problems, a hereditary issue which my mom and Mary got away with. That's the luck of the draw.

That meant too that us lads escaped it; if your mom doesn't have it, you don't have it. We were just fortunate and it makes you humble when you see how it affected other people in your family, who you were so fond of. My Auntie Eily and uncle Mickey had kidney issues all their lives, while Paddy died at 40 in 1980. And then, of course, there'd been my grandmother, who had passed away on a pilgrimage to Lourdes that she had taken because she was ill and dying.

Growing up, we were always so aware that there were medical complications with the Kavanaghs and how this thing that came from my mom's side filtered all the way down. We saw the effect it had. But with modern medicine now the next generation could have a totally different experience and outlook.

If people ever think of the Ó Sé story, they may remember signature moments like my brother Darragh fielding a high ball, Tomás soloing up the pitch, or all Páidí's heroics down the years.

But the women of the family equally made the name what it is. My grandmother Beatrice, for a start, was at the heart of everything at Ard an Bhóthair. She came from a huge family in Sligo and was very maternal, a proud lady and a bold entrepreneur. As well as that, she worshipped her youngest child, Páidí.

Her house at the crossroads was like a shrine to Páidí. People think that's just an expression, but if you walked in the door, you'd be greeted with pictures of Páidí. In her bedroom, the kitchen, the good room. All over the house – it was pictures upon pictures of Páidí getting awards, Kerry teams, photos of her youngest son with a visiting celebrity or politician.

She had two other sons, remember, and plenty of grandkids. But the only other person to get a look in on the walls was Padre Pio. It was just P.O. and Pio himself up on the wall, my father would say.

They kept Irish students over the years – even though, coming from Sligo and then living in England for some years, she hadn't the language herself. It didn't stop her. When the inspectors were coming around, she'd have to come away from being front and centre and put somebody else as the spokesperson. Páidí didn't necessarily get his roguish streak from the Ó Sé side.

Generally, she'd have a few stock phrases that she relied on and peppered into her chat, like, '*Cailíní*, upstairs, *anois* [Girls, upstairs, now],' and she got through fine with that. The students were very well looked after and learned from the great people she had around her. Páidí always said, and showed afterwards, it's important to delegate, as a manager.

Beatrice hired people to work there who would have been fluent in Irish and they'd be doing all the heavy lifting when it came to teaching the language.

As we were growing up, you'd be kicking ball outside her house up against the gable end of the church. It might be raining and you'd come in and visit her and she'd go over and she'd feel your arm.

'Oh my God, take off that pullover.'

And you'd have to put it up in the range and dry it off and you'd be sitting there and she'd be giving you a bowl of soup or a cup of tea and you'd be happy out watching TV amongst all these pictures of our legendary uncle.

She loved one drink then after her day's work, just a nice hot whiskey from the pub. She'd say to one of us young lads, 'Go over there and get my nightcap' and you'd have to go over across the road and ask in behind the counter for Beatrice's drink.

But when the legs got feeble and she couldn't go across the road herself I suppose she missed that side of it, though she had plenty of callers.

Later on, when we were playing for Kerry, we'd have various superstitions. And one of those little *piseogs* was to call into Beatrice before heading off to the game to say goodbye to her and you'd give her a *póg* on the cheek.

We were grown men at this stage going off to play for Kerry on the telly. But she'd take out her little purse and press a €5 note into Darragh's hand, she'd give Tomás €5 and she'd give me a fiver too. Then Páidí, the manager, would come in and she'd take €50 out of the purse and give it to him, with a good luck kiss.

Páidí was king and she drove that man to be successful. He couldn't do any wrong in her eyes.

There's a picture of Páidí that hangs – amongst many – in the pub in Ard an Bhóthair. He's in his 20s, posing in a Kerry jersey, looking down the lens, sheepishly. It now looks over the beer garden he later built, but for many years it hung in my grandmother's house on the other side of the crossroads. She often said it was her favourite.

High praise given the fact she could have filled the Louvre with pictures of her youngest child. But this one picture, in the entire shrine, had pride of place and she often reminded us it was her pick of the bunch. We'd say, 'Why is that, Gran?'

'Walk over there,' she'd instruct us in replying.

'Páidí's still looking at you,' she says.

And she'd have us walking to every corner of the room testing her theory. She was evidently up to this herself when on her own – walking around the room while maintaining eye contact with this portrait.

'Wherever you go,' she'd repeat, 'Páidí's looking at you. A small bit like the Mona Lisa.'

He was some Mona Lisa.

In 1984, Páidí was part of a West Kerry divisional side that won the Kerry championship for the first time since 1948.

South Kerry, featuring the likes of Páidí's inter-county teammates John Egan and Jack O'Shea, were beaten by a single score: 1–7 to 1–6. It would mean Páidí would be Kerry captain in 1985.

In March of that year, when I was running around Ard an Bhóthair as an almost-five-year-old, work started on the site across the road. Páidí instructed the builders he wanted to be pulling pints in his new pub within 10 weeks.

Charlie Haughey, then in opposition, had agreed to cut the ribbon on the pub though he urged Páidí to beat Cork in the upcoming Munster final first.

They did so and Páidí often mentioned how much the victory meant to him as captain. Though he did also always recall how he broke a light in the dressing rooms that day bouncing a ball. Of course, down the line, I'd get to know those low-ceilinged Páirc Uí Chaoimh dressing rooms so well too.

A few days later Steve Cooney and Séamus Begley provided the music and Haughey's helicopter landed on the field beside the pub before he did the honours. Páidí's was open at Ard an Bhóthair.

Every great team runs out of road. This was the second coming of Mick O'Dwyer's Kerry, of course. They'd won four during their first flourish and perhaps they would have taken the show off the road long before 1985 if they hadn't been sent on an enforced hiatus by Offaly and then Cork in 1982 and 1983.

Monaghan almost caught them in the semi-final in 1985, but they made it through with a draw. Páidí and Kerry refocused and the skipper played excellently in a replay, booking their place in the final once more.

Kerry beat Dublin in the championship finale and Páidí made a short acceptance speech *as Gaeilge* as Charlie Haughey sat behind his friend, smiling and applauding. The Sam Maguire was brought to the Haughey home at Kinsealy first and a few days later, carried over the threshold of the bar at Ard an Bhóthair.

It was a magical moment for everyone in Ventry and Ceann Trá. I was about five at the time and Páidí bringing Sam back to our people is one of my earliest memories.

While Páidí was playing, my grandmother brought in a caravan and placed it behind the family home.

By the time I was growing up, it was a wreck and he wasn't using it because he'd moved next door. I remember it as a place you'd fire stuff into for storage. But before that it served as a high-performance unit and a hideaway for Páidí while he was training.

Everything revolved around Páidí's regime. There's the story of the vet who came around 11 a.m. one day to test the animals and Beatrice told him to go away and come back in the afternoon. He might wake Páidí from his nap.

Though the season didn't start seriously until much later then, Páidí would do so much during the wintertime to keep himself ticking over. I vividly recall the likes of Ógie Moran doing that 14-mile track around Slea Head over the Clasach, the road that leads from Ventry to Dunquin.

They'd slog out these long runs but Páidí would also wrap up, adding extra layers on top, just to sweat it out more. He'd come home to the crossroads and Beatrice would have a steak searing in the pan. She'd have prepared a roasting hot bath upstairs with vinegar, which she reckoned was good for the muscles.

When Páidí was finished and he pulled himself out of

the tub, he sat up at the table for his steak, washed down with a glass of milk.

Look away now sports nutrition experts, but finally, he'd have a glass of sherry in the bath, which his mother swore was very good for his digestion and recovery as well. Marginal gains served in a sherry glass.

Beatrice was just determined to treat this man to everything he needed off the field so that he'd be excellent *on* the field. She had a huge influence on him, there's no doubt.

I used often to ask my dad and my uncle Tom about my grandad and they'd always say the same thing: a very quiet man. Maybe he knew that his wife was a force of nature and was able to mind things and had the capacity to run a business and rear a family and do all these things.

His health wasn't great and he never fully recovered from the accident in London, I think. Beatrice was very much the domineering partner of the two of them and was the bread winner, in those years, which must have been unusual in the Ireland of that time.

Páidí entered the Garda Síochána and was stationed in Limerick. He was suffocated by the lifestyle I think and later, when he left the force, he rented out Kruger's Bar in Dunquin – his first steps into business. I have no doubt that he would have had the benefit of a dig out from my grandmother to get things up and running.

CHAPTER 2

ONCE WERE BROTHERS

When Páidí was growing up, he would listen to Michael O'Hehir describe the likes of Down or Galway winning an All-Ireland and then race for a patch of land between the cross and Ventry strand.

The garden we had at the side of our house at Ard an Bhóthair was *our* Croke Park and the start of the road in terms of anything we achieved later.

The youngest in any family might often end up with great music taste or be exposed to movies a little early. Having three older brothers also teaches you how to look after yourself and sharpens any nascent skills, let me assure you.

We were lucky in that we had plenty of room to play and we spent hours on end between our poor mother's lawn, the churchyard or various patches of grass in the area. And with four of us brothers storming out the back door to the garden like it was the Hogan Stand tunnel, the games were neatly divided into a natural two v. two.

There were water pipes coming down the side of the house and one going horizontally across – they formed a perfect set of goalposts in our imagination. And the beauty about playing there was the side of the house was fairly tall too so, unless you ballooned it altogether, it more often than not came back to you. The gift of repetition.

In the first years, it was usually the eldest, Fergal, and myself against the pairing of the middle boys, Darragh and Tomás. This was when we learned the skills of the game: blocking, kicking, tackling. It was rich soil for our growth. It was also a prison-yard scrap at times and sharpened our edge.

I was only seven or eight playing against bigger lads. I'd stick at the task and be annoying and knacky and maybe that informed my game later on. But if I got a belt or was thrown around the place, I'd run in crying to my mother at the kitchen sink, inside the window.

Sulking for a while, I'd sit inside at the kitchen table feeling sorry for myself until inevitably one of the boys would come to the window and pull a face at me. That was enough to get the blood boiling again and I'd steam back out – which was what they hoped to achieve.

Fergal went on to be a Kerry minor – in fact, he captained the team – and was a very promising footballer. He won a county minor championship with West Kerry and then went on to play in midfield for the Kerry minors with Séamus Moynihan in the Munster final against Cork, who beat them.

I remember clearly being at the game watching Fergal in the famous green and gold jersey going up against these two giants Cork had in the middle of the park, Pat Hegarty and Fachtna Collins. It was an important moment for him but also for the rest of us too.

Fergal played in trial games with the Kerry seniors alongside the likes of Pat Spillane, a link back to Páidí's teams, and other Kerry greats who were still playing. He was in around the panel and was on his way to breaking through and establishing himself when he suffered a cruciate injury.

The timing was so cruel. He was only finding his way with Kerry, he hadn't made that breakthrough yet and he had to go off and do a recovery on his own, which made the thing that bit more difficult. The rehab with anterior cruciate ligaments is so different now compared to then. These days you get a programme; you follow it step-by-step like a recipe or a map.

But in the mid-1990s, that direction or support wasn't there and he was very much doing his own thing in the gym and didn't really have the guidance that you would need to come back as strong again. Seeing him in that Kerry jersey, though, had shown all of us the way.

Fergal then went off to Mary I College to study teaching, and the garden was a little less crowded under a dropping ball. With just the three of us left, we decided it was one in goal and two outfield.

We concocted various handicaps to level the playing field. The fact that I was the youngest dictated that if it was me v. Darragh, he'd only be allowed to solo with his left or we'd hamper him in some way.

The age difference between me and Tomás is negligible, and no quarter was asked or received. It set the tone for the rest of our lives really. It was some craic, sport for the pure love of it, but without us even realising, our skills were improving.

There was only football in our little *gort* and in west Kerry generally. Though there might well have been hurling if one man had succeeded in instilling it in the people a couple of generations before me.

Páidí's father-in-law, Stephen Fahy, grew up in Castlegar, just outside Galway city. A young member of An Garda Síochána, he was posted to the village of Camp, 10 miles west of Tralee. Castlegar was hurling country and the young policeman loved the game.

He hoped he could encourage a new passion in the young men of his new home on the Dingle Peninsula and tried to set up a hurling club. Despite his obvious enthusiasm, he soon learned nothing was allowed to interfere with football in this part of the world and the idea was left lie.

*

Páidí and Máire's kids, Neasa, Siún and Pádraig grew up next door, of course. It was an open-door policy and we all relied on each other; we were in and out. They're a lot younger than me. I was born in 1980. Neasa was born in 1988 and Siún in 1989 – the Irish twins. They're like sisters to us. Pádraig, the baby, came along a few years later – but they were practically reared in our house and vice versa.

Pádraig and his mother Máire are now driving things on with the bar and doing a great job; he's made changes and brought it forward again.

Though we come from a county with a rich footballing heritage, growing up when we did, those were actually Kerry's barren years.

Kerry beat Meath in 1986 in the last sting of Mick O'Dwyer's great team – with Páidí claiming his eighth medal – but Seán Boylan's Royals took over in 1987 and backed it up in 1988.

The rivalry between that Meath team of Mick Lyons, Colm O'Rourke and Liam Hayes, and Billy Morgan's upcoming Cork side defined that late 1980s era and I loved watching those matches. Cork of course got over the line in 1989 against Mayo and, crucially, beat Meath in 1990.

A lot of people talk about me and this thing with Cork, that we had this huge rivalry; of course we had a huge rivalry with Cork, but I actually grew up watching Cork in those years between 1987 and 1993 and loving that team. Some of the Cork players were my heroes. Some of the Meath players were my heroes.

Páidí had always swapped jerseys during his career and he used to stash them in his house. Of course, often when he wasn't around, we'd raid his collection, pulling on shirts of every colour to help re-enact whatever game we'd seen on TV. And any birthday or Christmas or if we'd saved a few bob, we'd spend it on jerseys. People might not believe me, but I'd often play in the red of Cork and pretend to be men like Larry Tompkins, Niall Cahalane and Stephen O'Brien – I admired them all.

I remember clearly sitting in front of the TV watching Cork and Meath and seeing Colm O'Neill coming up to Mick Lyons and giving him a bang into the jaw and I'm watching this thinking this is incredible. Mick Lyons just put his hand to his cheek and turned away, which was a really manly and sporting gesture in its own way. O'Neill was dismissed and Cork were down to 14 and yet they still won the match to complete the double of hurling and football All-Irelands. It was just amazing stuff to me, watching in west Kerry.

And like lots of kids, you're hoovering up as much information as you can with newspapers and magazines and asking your father about players and who was good in past days. I was a sponge. The privilege we had was the encyclopaedia that was Páidí, living next door.

One of the first games I attended was the Munster final in 1993. I couldn't see over the old crush barriers in Killarney despite straining on my tippy toes, so my dad caught me and lifted me over.

And the thing I took back out the gate with me was a real awe of Teddy McCarthy, who gave an absolute exhibition of high feeling on a beautiful day in Fitzgerald Stadium. He was just this superb midfielder who'd go up and catch a ball, and what I especially loved was that he leapt high into the sky to win these balls, while not being a huge giant. It was inspirational.

Here was this fella going up for balls that he had no right to win. And the Kerry–Cork thing, while there was a rivalry, it was respectful and it was a rivalry that you'd still appreciate greatness from the opposition.

The well-known Dublin legend Robbie Kelleher – who was a key part of the Heffo's Army era – purchased a summer house in Ventry around this time, overlooking the harbour, and he was good friends with his former opponent, Páidí.

The Kellehers had three boys, Kieran, Rory and Declan, and Robbie just threw the three boys into the garden often and we'd play our own Dublin–Kerry classics.

Another day, Listowel were playing a game back our way and the Kerry great Tim Kennelly and Páidí were over in the pub drinking porter all day long after the game. Tim's sons, Noel and Tadhg, fell in with us and would go on to be teammates of ours with Kerry in the future. We'd kick with anyone who was there. There's a great family photograph of my mom, my dad and the four of us boys, as well as the Cork hurling great Seánie O'Leary. Seánie would come down and stay in the house for the week with his wife, Geraldine, and children, Kieran, Aideen and Tomás.

When they stayed with us we played hurling for the week. The football was totally forgotten about, and we knew little of rugby. But in this photograph, you can see I'm sporting a nasty black eye.

During the week, Tomás caught a sliotar and hit me across the face inside in the bedroom and knocked me out. My mother arrived on the scene and asked what happened and, after coming around, I couldn't say. It was an omertà we often repeated in later scrapes.

Tomás, like he was up in front of the GAA's Competitions Control Committee, just denied it.

As boys who loved to play, I realise how privileged we were growing up. We were safe because my dad would just close all the gates if it was a busy weekend or the pub was hopping on a bank holiday.

We had a nice bit of a garden and it was a big house because we kept nearly thirty Irish language students during the summer. It was the perfect environment for us to play freely and get better while having fun – I know that's not the case with everyone.

*

Darragh went off next, leaving myself and Tomás at home with our parents. The little matches came to an end generally but we devised competitive skill competitions.

You might have to kick nine balls over the bar with your left leg and then your right leg. And there were three stations located throughout the garden – and our imaginations. Then there was another set of three further back and another layer deeper back the garden.

It was different when Darragh was gone, of course. It was less about little All-Ireland finals at 90 mph, but we were still competing and honing our skills in a different way.

I was obsessive – we concocted one game in which you'd hit one kick 13 yards out, one straight in front of the goal, one to the right, one to the left – and then we'd increase the distance. Some lads have a misspent youth in the snooker hall; we lost a lot of hours kicking a ball over a drainpipe.

A metal fire escape wrapped around the other gable end of the house. After these games, we'd pretend those stairs were the Hogan Stand steps and would hang over the balcony shaking an imaginary Sam Maguire.

We were privileged and the fact we had a roomy garden was a godsend and something that people take for granted. When you have a patch of grass where you can kick the ball and it comes back to you from the gable of the house or a wall, you're on to a winner. It's something people underestimate and we'll see the consequence of a dearth of playing areas for this generation in the future.

Sometimes, however, the ball didn't come back to you, as Páidí demonstrated one day when I was 10 years old …

One of those long summer days in 1990 we were in the garden kicking the ball between a handful of us, typically enough. Páidí crossed the road and informed us that word had reached him from Dingle that the Kerry icon, Mick O'Connell, from Valentia Island was on his way to visit Ard an Bhóthair. O'Connell, of course, invariably rowed himself across the water for training and matches during a stellar playing career that earned him a spot on the Team of the Millennium.

Keen to impress a true great of the game, Páidí gathered us around to give us instructions: 'This is how we'll showcase what the next generation has in west Kerry.'

Páidí turned to face the side of the church which had two stained-glass windows on the gable end and said we'd aim – and hit – the old bell in the middle. That will impress O'Connell.

To demonstrate, he stood back, set himself and took a shot at the bell. The ball smashed straight through one of the church's stained-glass windows. I can still hear the glass breaking now.

Game over.

Páidí said, 'Right lads, we'll go to the pub; we'll leave it off.' The window was destroyed as we ran across the road to the safety of Páidí's. When O'Connell arrived, Páidí got us to try to catch these high balls in front of the master of the art.

But of course, I was only small and I was struggling with the big O'Neill's Size 5 – I'd have to bring it into my chest, rather than hold it in my hands like Páidí wanted. Páidí took this in for a minute or so in front of O'Connell then grunted, 'That's no good,' and the two of them went off to the pub for the afternoon, with the broken stained-glass window behind us.

A few days later, the monsignor, Pádraig Ó Fiannachta – who was a cousin of my dad and Páidí – was speaking from the pulpit on the Sunday. I sunk into the pew, as he said, 'There are young fellas here in the crossroads, and they're running wild, causing damage and even destroying church property.' I was sitting there amongst the congregation, absolutely mortified though I'd not even committed the crime. As I was being read from the pulpit, Páidí, of course, was across the road in the house in bed, 10 toes up. Not a bother.

Páidí had an encyclopaedic knowledge of Kerry football's family tree and could speak at length on the topic of the generations of players who came before him and us. Perhaps it started in the shop at Ard an Bhóthair.

Batt Garvey, who it's said invented or at least perfected the solo run, would call in. Originally from Ventry, Batt won an All-Ireland in 1946 and was known for his skills in a tough era. He was ahead of his time.

A year after that All-Ireland win, he played in the famous

1947 Polo Grounds final between Kerry and Cavan, and Páidí would pepper the visitor with questions about that glamorous fixture, New York and those famous games.

When he made his visits to our crossroads, Batt would place a ball on a high windowsill of the shop front. 'Now, Páidí,' he'd say, 'you have to learn how to jump high and knock it off.'

Páidí said he practised this little skill repetitively afterwards in preparation for Batt's return to our homeplace, and Páidí did the same thing for me afterwards.

Our uncle insisted in later years that Batt had lamented the fact Páidí didn't come along sooner and the pair, from different footballing generations, could have kicked ball together growing up at the cross as contemporaries. I know there was a lot of respect and affection between them.

Another Ventry man, Mick Murphy, was also a footballing hero who was often referenced. He taught in our primary school – Cill Mhic an Domhnaigh – and there was huge pride in his achievements.

People from back in the road too made their way west and were mined for information and good conversation about Páidí's favourite topic, Kerry football. He loved discussing the old players and that chain through time was important to him. He got what it meant.

CHAPTER 3

FEAR AN TÍ

I'm not sure if the work ethic was passed on to the likes of Fergal, Tomás, Darragh and myself, but my mother is some woman to work. She has a work ethic like you'd never see. My mother is well past retirement age now but she is still up first thing in the morning looking after the place and the garden and it's still operating as a B&B. If something falls or something is broken, that's fixed the following day. There was a work ethic hardwired in. This is a lady who finished school at 12 when her mom died. She went on to become a nurse and made a life for herself and her family.

When we were growing up, during the summer, we'd keep 28 students – or the 'Gael Linns' as we called them – at a given time, with six bedrooms upstairs. You can imagine the chaos – and the work. We were, of course, expected to help in the running of the house – no more than serving up the students' *bricfeasta* each morning but that involved a bit more than pushing down a few slices of bread in the toaster.

My father had our two cows, which we'd have to milk ourselves. We'd then have to pasteurise the milk for the students' cereal. This involved letting the milk sit and waiting for the cream to form at the top. You'd clear that off … but then there'd be a second layer of cream.

Of course, we'd make a balls of it. You can imagine myself, Tomás, Darragh and Fergal as teenagers trying to pasteurise milk and pour out orange juice in front of these girls from Dublin or wherever. You know when Fr Ted realises he's left Dougal to 'do a funeral' and it cuts to the hearse on fire in the open grave? Not far off. We'd have a table full of students inside the dining room and they're looking at you saying, 'What the fuck is this?' as this lumpy milk plops out of the glass bottle into the bowl of cornflakes.

Every morning the beds were made and the place was cleaned and there was just so much work that went into those students, who we had for nine weeks of the summer.

In Ventry there was a real rhythm to our lives. That happens with people who are into or play sport anyway – the calendar is bookended by the start of a season and the end of a competition at the same time each year. So too we could mark out the months with various jobs. We loved bringing home the hay on the farm and it was great craic working together and messing.

But if there was a time of the year that we absolutely dreaded it was the day the students went out the door at the end of the summer, because my mother sprang into action. She'd have us lined up and ready for a day's hard labour. You'd have to go upstairs, dismantle every single bunk, then have to put up the double beds.

Us lads would be doing the heavy lifting but she'd have all this done in the space of one day, where you would dismantle every single bed, take them down. Then you'd have to put up all the double beds, which would have been stored away in the sheds and she would have the bed and breakfast sign up that evening. And she could have five rooms filled that evening for B&B.

The year my dad died then she completely pared back on the Gael Linns. It changed then.

So, as I said, if we ever got a work ethic, it would have been from my mom, as opposed to my dad. He rode in behind her and liked the easy life. She was very much the driving force; there's no doubt about that.

I'm still great friends with former Dublin footballer Alan Brogan, and I was at his wedding to his bride, Lydia, around ten years ago. I was behind enemy lines of course, surrounded once more by Dubliners.

Lydia leant over to me at one stage and said, 'I stayed

in your house; I remember you running around the kitchen.' I couldn't believe it.

'I used to keep to myself,' I explained, and admitted I didn't remember her at all.

It wasn't quite their honeymoon but later Alan and Lydia came back to Ard an Bhóthair and they called over to see my mom and they knocked great enjoyment out of reminiscing about those summer days. Lydia was brought for a tour of the place and could retrace her steps as a teenager and see the room where she stayed. The place was a big part of people's lives for a time each year.

A man we nearly call part of the family is Munster great, Mick Galwey. He lives over the ditch from our place – himself and his wife Joan have the summer house next door.

But at the start, Joan Corkery, from Millstreet, stayed in our house as a teacher, instructing the students for a few summers. She was learning her Irish herself as a young woman and of course her boyfriend, Galwey, came down to see her.

Jesus, my father and Galwey really hit it off. They became great friends.

As often happens in young relationships, though, Galwey went by the wayside for a while and things cooled off. We didn't see him around Ventry for a bit.

After a good while, Joan brought this other fella down

to meet us and see the place. We heard him coming before we saw him. He came down the road on this big, loud motorbike and stood it up in front of the house. You can imagine how impressed us boys were. We were all attracted out of the garden as if the Whippy Man was playing his ice cream jingle. He let us rev the engine and gave us spins around the crossroads on the back of the bike.

Throughout, my father stayed inside drinking his tea, half sneaking a look out the window at all the action. But he did not budge from the sitting room.

After a while this lad headed away on his bike and Joan, who would be a fairly assertive lady, came in the door and said to my father, 'My God, Michael, I thought you were very rude.'

My dad put down his cup of tea and said, 'Bring back Galwey.' Galwey was eventually brought back, of course, and the Galweys have been a big part of life in the crossroads for many years.

Like a lot of moms of that time, perhaps, my mother was in the background when it came to sport but was really supportive.

Darragh went on to be one of the most dominant midfielders in the game, but like the rest of us, he was a late developer. He'd be in the gym with a development squad rather than pasteurising milk these days perhaps.

He came home from a West Kerry game one evening and it was evident he hadn't got a game. My dad informed my mother quietly that Darragh was upset. But my mother went through the routine of washing the gear anyway, just to let on that he had played. She wouldn't mention the football team at all, but she just washed his gear anyway so that he wouldn't have to talk to her about it.

My mother would never go to the games – from when we started to when we finished up in Croke Park on Kerry's biggest days. She was too nervous and apprehensive, like a parent would be. As well as that, listening to people in the stands, making thoughtless remarks about the players they're judging or, worse, shouting abuse at the young teams – that would have been tough.

From years of sitting next to him watching my elder brothers, I know that's something that cracked my dad up, but he never opened his mouth. I'm not sure how I'll react to people's bluster if I end up in my father's position. I'll remember him and count to ten, I'd like to think.

My mother's approach to taking in our games was no different to my grandmother, Beatrice, before her. My mother wouldn't go into a game to watch it in person ever but might have a Kerry match on the radio as she did her jobs around the house.

She'd sit down and watch *The Sunday Game* that night and she'd certainly have an opinion on a player or if someone was getting carried away with themselves. She wouldn't be long telling you that fellas were getting a bit too big for their boots – the implicit message to us was clear and I think we brothers were all conscious of staying grounded.

Beatrice often put Páidí's mucky Adidas boots outside the door after a big game and, in the days before inter-county kit men, the gear would be on the line.

In our house, after a Munster final our mother would have the No 2, the No 5, and the No 8 jerseys up on the clothesline at Ard an Bhóthair, having done the laundry again. She was proud of us in her quiet way.

Tom Long, a first cousin of my father, was a real touchstone for us growing up. He set the standard before Páidí even, and the stories of his exploits were well rehearsed in Ard an Bhóthair.

He won two All-Irelands with Kerry, playing, in 1959 and 1962, in key central positions with skill and courage. We were proud of all the Longs, especially Tom and the fact that he was the first of our family to win senior All-Irelands.

My father told me once that when Páidí won his first All-Ireland medal in 1975, a neighbour from Ard an Bhóthair remarked that 'The Ó Sés will no longer live under the shadow of the Longs anymore.' A big statement.

The point was that with my uncle Tom first winning an All-Ireland minor medal and then, more notably, Páidí winning his first senior title, it was as though we had now cemented our own name. Because the Long name meant a lot.

Tom died recently and I of course attended his funeral. There were a lot of men there who would have been the same vintage as my father.

There were some old black and white pictures from the Sem school teams with all these young faces looking back at you. It was poignant. They were a great generation of men, some of them still going strong thankfully; others, like my father, are gone now. I was looking around the room and it struck me that now we are the new representatives of the family, when one of these men caught my hand and said, 'Jesus, there's a huge show of support from the Ó Sés tonight.'

We might be scattered all over – I'm in Tralee, Fergal's at Ard an Bhóthair, Darragh in Tralee and Tomás in Cork – but we all arrived in dribs and drabs, knowing it was important.

Tom Long left the Gaeltacht, taking up a teaching post in Killarney and he left the club, An Ghaeltacht. But he was somebody who we were always so proud of. He was a Kerry great. People remember special names like Mick O'Dwyer, Mick O'Connell, that great era for our county – but you also talk about Tom Long.

Some people in the generations that came later associated Tom Long with Killarney and didn't realise he was a proud Ventry man too. Oftentimes I'd be in company and Tom's name would come up in conversation about great Kerry players of the past and our connection would be referenced. Invariably someone would say, 'Jeez, I didn't know that; Tom Long is related to you?' And I'd be proud to say, he was.

CHAPTER 4

MEITHEAL

Build it and they'll come. Páidí's bar attracted the best traditional musicians to our back yard, but I remember when it was all fields. The area across the road from the shop was called Patchin's Field.

'Who's going to the field kicking ball?' was the refrain. It was a ditch and you'd climb over and we were going in there so often that the grass was bare and we played football in there. Little did we know that was where Páidí was going to build a legacy afterwards.

Páidí entered the Garda Síochána training college at Templemore in May 1975. He often joked the entrance exam was the only test he ever passed. I'm sure that wasn't true.

He was stationed in Limerick city and he was looked after by Kerry man John Costello, who was very good too to Tomás when he was at Mary Immaculate in the city many years later.

Páidi used to tell a story of one night when John and himself were cruising around Limerick in a patrol car. News of a possible bomb came across the radio so John quickly threw the car around.

'What are you doing?' Páidí asked him.

When John replied he was heading towards the bomb, Páidí replied: 'What do you know about explosives?'

The men decided they'd stay out of harm's way in the end.

Longing for home and maybe stifled by the structure of the police force, Páidí made the ballsy decision to throw his garda cap at it. He'd been thinking about this career change for a while and planning accordingly. He often hinted that his supervisors didn't exactly try to convince him to stay – playing for Kerry was very much his priority then, not filling a charge sheet.

In 1977, he convinced a bank manager to give him a loan to buy that patch of land across the road from the family shop at Ard an Bhóthair. A year later, he applied for planning permission to build a pub but was refused – the rationale was that the area had enough public houses.

It might have been a blessing in disguise. He leased Kruger's Bar in nearby Dunquin instead and served an apprenticeship as a publican there. He left the gardaí in 1979.

It was there that he first got to know Fianna Fáil leader and Taoiseach Charlie Haughey, who owned the nearby island of Inishvickallane. They first met at Easter in 1980 and Páidí learned a lot from him as Haughey introduced

Páidí to businesspeople and tourism experts. They were an odd couple but they had an enduring friendship afterwards.

The pub was popular anyway and people started to travel there because Páidí was well known as a Kerry footballer too. He learned his trade there and then he made the final step home, to build the pub in 1985.

There were a lot of objections at the time from locals – like from the neighbouring pub across the way, which was owned by Paud Quinn. It was understandable if he thought this new establishment might take from his business. The community was split and you can imagine it was stressful.

As it transpired, Páidí and Paud Quinn became good friends afterwards and worked in collaboration – there was plenty to go around.

After the pub was built, Páidí built on as he went along. The beer garden was added, then it was enclosed and the pub became a destination for people out for a spin around the Slea Head for their holidays.

The bar was jointed. I will never forget coming home from school on Mondays and the place would be hopping. Mondays were bonkers in the pub. Drinkers were serious drinkers back then.

But Sunday would be even busier because Cooney and Begley would be there.

I ended up playing the accordion with these legends but we started off on the piano.

There was a lady up the road from our house, Stephanie Holstead, who was a piano teacher. Fergal escaped for some reason, but us three had to attend for lessons.

Darragh would cycle up with me on the carrier and Tomás would have his bike. My parents paid for the hour's lesson so we each got 20 minutes of one-on-one tuition. Tomás then went to Teach Siamsa, where you'd learn all sorts like sean-nós – the old Irish singing.

You'd learn the *feadóg stáin* (the tin whistle), you'd learn the accordion and that's where the accordion started off for me. Because I was showing a bit of interest and a flair for the accordion, my parents sent me further into Dingle to Pat Nelligan, who was also my history teacher later in Dingle CBS. I had lessons with him every Saturday morning and we took it from there.

My father got me an expensive new accordion – a Paolo Soprani – which was worth around a grand, a chunk of change now and even more money then. It was a big deal to get it and meant I had to commit.

We'd go into Pat Nelligan on a Saturday morning and he'd play a tune from a musician, be it a well-known player like Bobby Gardiner or Joe Burke or whoever, and he'd have the song written out.

When I went in there first, I was learning off a half a verse each week, and then I'd come back the following week and play that nervously.

But eventually I'd be able to play that tune with my eyes

closed, knowing it off by heart. I wouldn't even have to look at the notes and then I'd play another half the next week and then before I knew it, I was coming back the following week and I'd have the tune off. Like kicking an O'Neill's off the side of the house with a certain leg from a certain spot and seeing improvement, similarly, I enjoyed the process of repeating the tune I was given, seeing improvement and ultimately nailing it.

As years went on, I was going in and learning three or four tunes per day when I was inside there. Soon I was picking up tunes by ear and it was becoming second nature. I loved the music and the tradition that was being passed down and really enjoyed the practice of it.

I did music for my Junior Cert as well, even though the subject wasn't even being taught in the school. I had to go up to the convent and get grinds once a week from a man and then just sit the exam. It was just one session per week and I still did well in the test, getting a B or a C. So, with my father's encouragement in particular, I carried it on. Did it help my football? I think in contrast to my efforts on stage, it showed me I was a more natural sportsman.

I was competing in Oireachtas competitions and other *feiseanna* around the place. One day I went to a competition in Killarney and my mom came with me, which was unusual. I went up on the stage to play my piece in front of the audience and judges … and I just froze.

I couldn't think of the tune.

It reminded me of the young lad on stage in *About a Boy*. He's on his own and is absolutely murdering 'Killing Me Softly' in front a packed school hall. Hugh Grant rescues him by running on stage and joining him in singing. There was no Hugh Grant for me.

I came off the stage, embarrassed and confused: *What just happened there?*

When I was about 16, I got into the habit of taking the keys to Páidí's fine big Renault Laguna and heading off around the parish for a spin.

He knew my uncle Mike had taught me how to drive and he was happy enough to see me edge out the gate in the evening time for an hour.

One evening in December, I called for a friend up the road, Peter Fenton, and as was our habit, he hopped in and we headed off for a spin. It was a school night during fifth year and we reckoned we deserved the study break. I could feel the power of this thing as I took it back up to Ard an Bhóthair and turned again.

We were heading straight on and Peter says there was no way I could have been thinking about turning left at an upcoming crossroads because we were trucking steadily. But at the last second, I said, 'Watch this now. I have this turn mastered here,' and threw it into the corner.

We ended up careering straight into a field, narrowly missing a big telephone pole. How did I miss it? I don't know, but we would have been stone dead. As the dust settled, I said, 'Peter, we're in a bit of bother here.'

We tried to get the car out of the ditch but it was too far in. We decided we'd have to go back up the road and ask a neighbour, P.J. Garvey, to pull us out. Our evening suddenly very stressful, we were sprinting up the road when a car started coming against us. We hopped into the ditch so we wouldn't be found out.

As we peered out of the undergrowth, we saw it was a neighbour, Joe Bán O'Shea. Thank God he was as blind as a bat because he went up to the pub, ordered a pint and says, 'Jesus, someone's after crashing a car out on the road and put it into the fields.'

We got the car pulled out, but as I was driving it back up the road, I knew we were in big trouble because it was steering like a wonky shopping trolley you'd get in the supermarket.

A couple of hours later, I saw Páidí coming out of the pub after his few pints and he was heading for the house. I'd been waiting for him and approaching him in tears, confessing, 'Páidí, I'm sorry but I'm after crashing the car.'

He looked at me and said, 'Look, don't worry about it, it's fine; we'll deal with it in the morning, once you're alright.' Then the blackmailing started …

I was making my few bob playing music in the pubs around the place and I was preparing to head off one evening soon after the visit to the ditch in the Renault.

Páidí stuck his head around the door and said, 'Come here, you have to work in the pub tonight.'

I said, 'I can't. I'm playing music in Ballyferriter.'

And he replied, 'You're working in the pub tonight, or else I'll be going into your parents.'

'Alright, alright, alright.' I had to pull out of the music gig that evening and subsequently, I never spent as many hours in the pub as I did that Christmastime. After a few weeks of this, I was fed up with the whole thing and he came back one evening and said, 'Come on over, you're working late.'

I said, 'I'm not Páidí.'

'You're coming over working tonight or else I'm telling your parents,' he said.

I blurted out, 'Do you know now, Páidí? You can fucking tell them. Because I've already told my parents. So, forget about it!' I'd had enough and his bubble was burst. He broke out laughing when I told him.

I got a small suspension – which wouldn't be my last, admittedly – off the parents; I didn't get to drive a car when I turned 17, as I had been expecting. I was made to wait until a few months later as punishment.

When the pub was full of music on a Sunday night, my parents would leave me slip in for an hour. I'd sit quietly watching these giants of their craft lift the roof off the place and the effect it would have on the crowd.

Then when Begley would want to take a break – he'd

slip his famous accordion onto me, squeezing a glass Coke bottle between the straps and my back so it sat properly and I was able to play. Then we were off.

I'd plug into this powerful machine with this amazing group of musicians and people would be shouting and roaring and swamping pints.

As Tommy Tiernan said, 'Jazz is about one person getting up on stage and saying, "I'm mad, take it or leave it." Irish trad is a lot more inclusive. Era fuck it *a mhac*, we're all mad, come on.'

They *were* mad nights. As it got later in the evening, I'd be told to head away and I'd go over the road home and straight in to annoy Tomás, bragging that I'd been admitted because I was with the band.

It was crazy stuff and a huge education to be growing up there and watching the different personalities coming in, the farmers and the fishermen and people from around the country. You got a sense of people.

Cooney and Begley were world famous; they were at the top of their game as a partnership then and toured the globe together. This odd couple – a box player from west Kerry and this hippy Australian guitar and didgeridoo player – released what's considered a seminal Irish album *Meitheal* in the early 1990s. The title refers, of course, to the practice of neighbours cooperating to bring in crops, build houses, look after animals.

To see the likes of them produce this magic was a privilege, and they were so kind and encouraging to me. The

Begleys are such a well-known traditional music family and are neighbours to us. They're as passionate about music as we'd be about football.

Páidí loved to survey this scene as the music ratcheted up. He had a huge appreciation for traditional music. He loved Begley and Cooney and he wanted to make Páidí Ó Sé's the place for authentic traditional music.

Every Sunday night, without fail, the place would be jam-packed because people knew Begley and Cooney were playing.

As well as the two lads, Páidí made sure he got in the best musicians around – Johnny Reidy from Scartaglen, Liam O'Connor, a renowned Killarney musician, Joe Burke, who was probably the best accordion player ever, down from Galway.

Later, I'd ask Cooney when he was passing through if I could play a few tunes with him. It was daunting as well as thrilling. Despite his bravado and charm, Páidí was shy behind it all. I'd be the same. People used to laugh at me when I was playing the accordion in the pubs because I was too shy to look out to the audience. I was almost turned into the wall to play the tunes.

I was playing away in Murphy's Pub in Ballyferriter one time and Nora, the owner, came out to me and said, 'Will you ever turn around towards the crowd.'

I said, 'Go 'way Nora, I'm lucky to be here at all.'

Like a lot of people who are quiet or shy in their earlier years, I've become more confident and I push myself out there more but, by nature, I think I'm a shy person still.

When it came to playing football, however, I was never shy and could express myself unselfconsciously. Maybe that was the difference between music and football for me. I look at my small fella, Tadhg, now and I think he's shy as well.

When I was playing the music, I loved it, but I was working overtime to stay at the pace and fit in.

One night there was a big event in Páidí's – TG4 were celebrating their 20-year anniversary on New Year's Eve. The station planned to broadcast live from the bar and I was down to go on with Séamus Begley. A big deal.

Like anything in television, it ran over and they were late getting to us, so I had a pint and I asked, 'What time are we on it?' Next thing I had the second pint. As we waited, we settled into it and it wasn't long before we had the gallon drunk.

The next thing they said, 'Right, come on, we're on!' Myself and Séamus Begley hopped up and we were playing away and despite being in front of a live crowd and a TV audience at home, I was totally relaxed.

I didn't care who was listening. I didn't care if it was on every TV in every living room throughout the country. It didn't bother me high up or low down. I needed the Dutch courage for the music – the thing is, the playing itself may have suffered.

I drifted away from music as I grew older as a teenager. If I'm honest with myself now, a lot of the reason why that happened was because there was almost a stigma when I was young about playing the music.

I had three elder brothers who cast a long shadow and I was always conscious of living up to my surname. The fact that I was becoming known as a musician gave people a pigeonhole to slot me: musician rather than footballer.

The jibe that Fergal, Darragh and Tomás were the footballers and I was the musician stung me. It was a perception that clawed away at the inside of me and cracked me up.

The result was that I decided I didn't want to be associated with the music and was instead determined to show people that I was a footballer in my own right. I still loved the music but it took a back foot simply because I knew football was number one anyway and it was what I wanted.

After Kerry won the All-Ireland in 1997, the Stacks player Pa Laide landed in at Ard an Bhóthair with the Sam Maguire, bringing it back to Páidí after a function. It was a friendly joke, which he's referenced to me in the years since, but Pa turned to me and said, 'And I hear you're going to win an All-Ireland too, Marc … in the music.'

CHAPTER 5

GROWING PAINS

Our name entitled us to certain privileges but made some demands too. It was brilliant to grow up around GAA legends – to see what it took to win All-Irelands, the commitment needed and the rewards of your work.

The price of that was the pressure to continue the chain. It was for me. I put myself under heavy pressure in my minor football year. Huge pressure. It was a year when I developed physically. I was small up until 16, even 17, though I was starting to grow and then at 18, I grew a good bit. I was going well enough but I was feeling the strain.

I had soaked up all the stories of Kerry greats, saw what it meant and watched my brothers start to make their way along the same path. I had this hang-up about making it as a minor like those who'd gone ahead of me.

As I've said, my uncle Tom won an All-Ireland minor medal in 1963. He was the first Ó Sé to play in Croke Park – he started it all for us. Kerry beat Westmeath 1–10 to 0–2 and the victory was a huge source of pride in the house at Ard an Bhóthair. He would always have boasted the fact that he was the only Ó Sé to win a minor medal.

Páidí had a heroic minor career but ballooned a penalty over the bar against Cork in a Munster final. He didn't do things by half. In fact, so much was a young P.O. earmarked for greatness that the county board brought him and Pat Spillane on a trip to Dublin to watch the 1972 All-Ireland final against Offaly. They failed to make the train home and instead spent some time kicking passes to each other in a deserted Croke Park that evening.

Fergal was captain of the Kerry minors, Darragh was a very good Kerry minor and I watched Tomás put in amazing performances at the grade over two years. My God, he played against Cork in a Munster final in 1996 at centre back and gave a performance for the ages – just reading the play so well, coming out with ball; he was just outstanding.

Páidí was manager of the senior team at this stage and after Tomás's performance we watched his team earn a breakthrough win over the Rebels. As I watched it, I was still thinking about the minor game, however, and said to myself, *That's the level I must train to get to.*

But I didn't get to that level at minor. I'd lie in bed at night thinking about what I needed to do, going over it in my mind and just piling pressure on myself to get on that Kerry minor team for a start. I put that onus on myself – it certainly wasn't coming from my parents.

I just had this thing, *What if I don't make the minors? I'll be seen as a failure. All my brothers have made it.*

I was in and around the panel and the first game we were playing was against Waterford, who had a strong team at the time, and the XV was being called out in the River Island Hotel in Castleisland while we were having some food after training. I was completely on edge and just praying to myself that I'd be in the starting side.

When I wasn't in the first 15 names announced, I hopped into the car, turned it towards Ventry and cried all the way home. I could not believe it.

We drew with Waterford as I watched on from the bench. It was a shocking performance and even though it was a good Waterford team, Kerry teams expect to win those games at any grade and there was war afterwards.

As often happens, I got wind the following night from someone in the know: 'You're going to be in the next day.'

And as it happened, for the replay in Austin Stack Park, I was wing back, a position I knew well. Jesus Christ, was there ever a man more relieved than me playing wing back. I felt comfortable and was doing okay but suddenly, I found myself pushed back into the full back line.

God Almighty – I'd never played in that position in my life. And I was bricking it because now I was the last line of defence. My head was full of thoughts: *What if a ball comes in here now? Where should I be standing?*

But I managed to coast through it without any major problems and we won. In the Munster final I did well against Limerick, again a good team. I was marking a fellow who went on to be a rugby international, Jeremy Staunton, who was a big, strong fella.

At one stage I went to shoulder him – let him know you're there! – and he kind of harrumphed, like an elephant irritated by a smaller creature. 'How dare you shoulder me?' was the vibe he gave off. But I got through it.

In the All-Ireland semi-final, we faced Laois and I probably had my best game. I was marking a fella called Brian McCormack, who was way bigger than me again. There were one or two balls that came in though and I got up over his head to catch them and came out with it.

You can find the footage in some dark corners of YouTube and I'm only skin and bone really. During the second half I made a few clearances in pure old-school football catch-and-kick style. I evidently did not care where that ball was going once it was away from me.

Páidí's Kerry were playing Mick O'Dwyer's Kildare the same day in the All-Ireland senior semi-final. The hype was intense. Charlie Nelligan, our manager, warned us beforehand that this place was going to be a sea of white for Dwyer's team – they'd be carrying the day.

'So,' he advised us, 'if you're kicking into the Canal End

or into Hill 16, you're not going to see the goal posts.' I was preparing to play wing back. I didn't think I'd be going up that far anyway, but when we were warming up, you could see this wave of whitewashing into the Hill as people made their way into the stadium.

I remember saying, 'Yeah, Charlie is right here; this is going to be hard to kick in against this backdrop.' And particularly so for me – I'm colour blind. I have difficulty telling the difference between navy and green or certain other colour combinations but it never really affected me later while playing for Kerry. It's more likely to be a slight annoyance when I sit down to watch a game of soccer on TV.

But I remember coming out at half time from the old dressing rooms under the Nally Stand. My legs felt heavy and Mikey Sheehy, an all-time great and Kerry selector on the day, had a word with me. 'Bursting out, Marco!' was his instruction.

They were words of encouragement from a Kerry icon, who went on to be a great friend of mine – because I think he saw here was a young fella who needed a word.

We lost by a point. But what an experience to play for Kerry in Croke Park on what was my first time. I was disappointed, of course, but I'd held up my part of the bargain with my family – in my head at least. I didn't hang onto too many jerseys in subsequent years but I still have that Adidas one.

In the days before that game, my uncle Tom, who was so proud of his minor pedigree, brought me into Tralee and dressed me up in a pair of slacks and a shirt and a jumper because that was his gig – the minors.

He took me into Seán Hussey's – one of the best places for clobber, as Tom would call it, and paid for all my clothes. I could tell he was proud and I felt so ready to go out onto the field and just do everything for him.

The main emotion I felt as we headed out the gate – on a day when the senior side ultimately lost to Kildare – was relief. Relief that I was on the team and I wouldn't go down as a failure.

On the outside, I might have come across as cocky but inside that very much wasn't the case. I was full of doubt and insecurity. But that day and that year had an important effect on my confidence and helped me realise that I was good enough.

As I've said, my father was a quiet man and wouldn't say much to us about football. But he did love going to the games and the thrill of watching us play.

I have treasured memories of going up to Dublin in 1997 and 2000 for All-Irelands with Darragh at the centre of a Kerry team rejuvenated by Páidí. We used to go up there and stay with cousins of ours, the Cruises in Crumlin.

Kerry got the job done in 1997, ending a relative famine – 11 years without Sam. The traditional banquet was held in the Burlington Hotel that night and it was the place to be. But we couldn't get in to see everyone, spend time with Darragh and enjoy the atmosphere.

My father was outside in the main bar having a few pints and it wouldn't have been in his nature to push himself forward. The last thing he would have wanted to do would be to feel like he was annoying Páidí or Darragh on their big night.

But I eventually got fed up with this and said, 'This isn't right at all, Dad. I'll get us in.'

I was only 17 and brave out. You know the way you see the American politicians slip in through the hotel kitchen after a speech in the movies? I went around to the back of the hotel, darted in the door between the hot stoves, through the chefs and porters and got into the big banquet hall. I was able to find Darragh, catch a hold of his shirt sleeve and say, 'Hey, get out here quick to get us in,' which he did.

We ended up having a great night inside and it was lovely then to see the players and be part of the night. It's something my dad got a kick out of.

He was probably more like his father before him than Páidí – and nothing really like his youngest brother in personality or features. My father wouldn't have given his opinion unless he was asked. He was a simple man who lived for his family and enjoyed his couple of pints on a Saturday or Sunday night around Dingle and at Páidí's after a week's work.

As the youngest, I'd often be with him at games while my older brothers were playing in big games. He'd be there to quietly support us but wouldn't roar at any of the lads. He'd let the boys do their thing. He'd be very nervous at games though. I'd sit next to him and the boys would get the ball and suddenly, his knee would push your leg and it was pure nerves. Then the boys would give off the ball and he'd relax again. But he was far from someone who was completely focused on football. He taught us the importance of other things too.

He was the one in the house who was very much focused on us and our education. In 1999, I repeated my Leaving Cert and Jack O'Connor asked me into the Kerry U21s.

But my father wouldn't allow me because he wanted me to focus on the exams.

Not that I would have made a difference if I was there, but Kerry lost the All-Ireland U21 to Westmeath. That was how serious he was about us getting an education and us doing well.

He regularly checked the homework to see was it of standard and, though we certainly weren't wealthy, he had no issue stretching to pay for grinds or whatever was needed to help with school, once we were seen to be trying.

It was him too, more than my mother, who pushed me with the accordion when I was growing up and when he realised I was decent enough at it, as I've said, he got me lessons and then that lovely and expensive Paolo Soprani accordion.

He was constantly making sure that our standards were high enough. He just wanted to see us do well and took a lot of quiet satisfaction if we did do okay. He was very proud, but nobody outside would see that pride. Maybe it's the old-school Irish male thing, but he'd tell my mom if we did well, but he wouldn't even tell us.

At one time when I was 16 years old or so, I played two games in the same week; in the first match I was outstanding. Everything just went for me and it was the best game I played all year – those days happen sometimes.

I came out of the game and I couldn't wait to get home and speak to my dad about it. I came in the door and said, 'Well, how do you think I got on?'

All I got was: 'You did grand.'

You did grand? I went out the door completely deflated. But the second day I played poorly, couldn't kick it straight or catch the ball, and I asked him again afterwards, 'Well, what did you make of that?'

Again, the reply was, 'You did grand.' He wasn't going to say it was great or he wasn't about to say I was shite.

It's not a bad approach. But he could get cross too. There was one time Tomás got sent off, like Tomás was capable of doing, and we were coming back from the game in silence in a tension-filled car.

After a period of silence and contemplation, my father turned to Tomás in the car, half puzzled, and asked, 'Tomás, what *ails* you?' He was perplexed. What drives you so mad? What is wrong with you? I was sitting in the back, delighted that it wasn't me this time.

He pushed us – but more in education than football. He was smart enough to realise that we didn't need pushing there and maybe a bit of balance was required.

I look at myself now with my small fella, Tadhg. He has basketball on Wednesdays, he's got soccer on Saturdays, he goes to Stacks for football. He plays football and other sports with his little pals and I'm watching him and I can feel myself getting frustrated. I see certain habits or little mistakes which all are to be expected at that age and absolutely part of learning the game. I try to think of my dad and what he would do. It's a powerful role model to still have.

God knows we tested my father's patience, though.

During my last year in school, for some reason, I put down computer programming on the CAO form. I got into Cork Institute of Technology – CIT – and was looking forward to college life but I'd not been doing the course a week when I knew I'd made a big mistake here. This was not for me.

The stuff we were doing was completely alien to me – new computer languages, maths, the days were 9 a.m. to 6 p.m., with just one break from 1–2 p.m.!

Ard an Bhóthair – where it all began. This is where my grandfather and grandmother set up a home and it's the place I still consider home to this day.

Páidí certainly did things in style. No less than former taoiseach Charlie Haughey flying in by helicopter for the opening of Páidí's pub in 1985.

Being held by my grandmother Beatrice with my grandfather Tommy by her side. Páidí's caravan is behind us – his 5-star hotel.

Family portrait for Darragh's holy communion. Tomás did a right number on me with Seánie O'Leary's hurley, knocking me out. The evidence is there to see with the black eye and the tears on my shirt. And look at the guilty head on Tomás!

Playing in the garden with the boys and our neighbour Mikey Cussen. We always had great fun out there and I've good memories of days like this.

Two little boys, myself and Tomás, playing with our tractors under the watchful eye of my dad in the background.

With Tomás on a rare trip to Dublin, taking in Dublin Zoo.
Getting the train up was an exciting time for us.

With Tomás and Dad at the pier, and the Great Blasket Islands in the background.

An old An Ghaeltacht photograph in Páirc an Ághasaigh, Dingle in the 70s. My dad (front row, far left) and my uncle Tom (front row, four from the left) both played on the day, alongside the great Mícheál Ó Sé.

Receiving an U12 medal from probably the three most influential people in my career: Liam Ó Rócháin, far right, Páidí in the middle and, of course, Mícheál Ó Sé, far left.

Dad took a sick day to go to the Irish Open in Ballybunion. Little did he know he would be on the front page the following morning as Tom Watson teed off. He got rightly caught!

When Tom Cruise was in the area filming *Far and Away*, Páidí made it his mission to get him to visit the pub – and, of course, he succeeded.

There are plenty of words to describe my uncle, these maybe aren't the first that come to mind. One of the quirkier features on the pub wall.

I'm not sure what I expected when I chose computer science all those months previously but I got a rude awakening and I'd advise any young person now to do some research before making those big decisions.

I knew I was on the wrong track and when I came home to Ard an Bhóthair, I went into my dad and said, 'Listen, I'm after making a mistake here.'

'Stick it out,' my father said. 'You'll be fine.'

I said, 'Look, no, honestly, I'm after making a mistake here. This course isn't for me.'

'Stick it out,' he repeated and that was it.

I struggled to get a handle on the subjects and was miserable. Predictably, I quickly got sick of going in there for full days and I got in the habit of hanging around the student house a lot, living the college life – apart from the academic work – going out at nighttime with the lads, sleeping in, training with my football team.

The time went by quickly enough in Cork and at the end of the year, we had six exams.

I actually passed two of them. Don't ask me how, but I scraped through a couple. The others? I failed three fair and square, and I didn't show up at all for one of them.

Liam Hodnett was the main man for football in CIT at the time and my father, hearing I'd failed a test or two, said, 'Will you arrange a meeting; we'll get Liam to get the top man in the computer course to have a word with you.'

My father came all the way up to Cork city and the two

of us went down to meet this guy. He was sitting there in an office and he started going through the results on a screen.

'Right, the six exams – you passed business. Well done.'

An encouraging start to the meeting.

'Computer applications,' he continued. 'You didn't even show up to this one, along with the three others that you failed. Where were you for computer applications?'

'Jesus,' I said. 'I must have had a football game that day,' I spluttered.

With that, my father just got out of the chair, 'Listen, sorry for wasting your time. What's the quickest way out of here. We'll be gone.'

That few minutes from the office to the car was the longest walk ever, knowing how disappointed he was and feeling that I'd let him down.

CHAPTER 6

COLLEGE MAN

The following university year things clicked. I was sent up the country to Maynooth and I was delighted. I hit it off because I loved the college, which was beautiful and small enough yet a decent size at the same time.

I was away from friends in Cork or Limerick, which was the other option on the table, and the course suited me much better: History. As well as that, the footballers there read like an inter-county team.

Dublin's Alan and Bernard Brogan and Barry Cahill, Mayo's Alan Dillon (who's now a government minister), Rory Kavanagh from Donegal, Colm Parkinson of Laois, John Keane (an All Star from Westmeath), Ross Munnelly (an All Star from Laois) and Roscommon's Paul Noone.

It was a serious team and we resolved to have a right go at the Sigerson Cup, the highly prestigious third-level football competition.

One of the biggest regrets, through all my football career, was not winning it.

That time the three games were on the one weekend. We played Sligo who were going for three in a row. It was a draw at full time, a draw after extra time, again after a second period of extra time, and we beat them by a point in the end.

But we were exhausted in the semi-final against Galway, who had the likes of Dessie Dolan, Joe Bergin and Michael Meehan. We had nothing in the tank and they beat us by three or four points.

Though we didn't win the big one during my three happy years there, Maynooth was like Barcelona's La Masia for inter-county footballers. Colm 'Wooly' Parkinson, who'd win a Leinster title under Mick O'Dwyer around this time, was also part of our academy.

Who could forget him? An excellent, if temperamental forward, he was hilarious.

At the start of the year, Willie Hughes who ran the football programme in the college sat us down in the dressing room and said, 'Right lads, this is the gear for the year; it's 25 quid each. You've got your jersey with your squad numbers, your shorts and socks.'

Everyone was agreeable but Wooly put up his hand, 'Hang on now a minute, Willie, I'm not paying any 25 pound for the gear. Why should I do that?'

'If you're not going to pay £25,' he was told, 'you can't play.'

'Well,' Wooly said, 'I don't think I will play then, Willie.' Everyone exploded laughing. We nearly did a whip around for him.

He almost led a full-scale strike over this custom that had been in place for generations. I'm sure we all ultimately coughed up and they let Wooly off quietly. He was an important player.

Anyone who has followed his broadcasting and podcasting career in recent years knows Colm's well able to make his point and argue a position.

There was another day we were on the way back to the training pitch outside Maynooth on the minibus after a game. It was a Thursday night and we were all looking forward to heading out afterwards and Wooly was at the centre of the craic.

He was joking and laughing loudly, and the bus driver turned to me at one stage and said, 'If he doesn't shut the fuck up back there, he's getting thrown off and he won't be going to any place later.'

I was the captain at the time and I said, 'Colm, quieten down a small bit, this man is going to throw you out.'

But Wooly got louder.

I said, 'Colm, shut the fuck up, will you?'

That had no effect either. There was steam coming out of the driver's ears at this stage and he threw the bus into the side of the road and roared at Wooly to 'get the fuck out'.

I'd seen this kind of bluff from my parents, teachers and coaches down through the years and thought an apology from Wooly would get us all back on the road.

'You're going to leave me here?' Wooly asked, looking hurt.

'We're going to leave you here unless you shut the fuck up,' the driver explained.

No deal. Wooly got off, the bus drove off down the road and there was no Colm at training that night.

Another night we played a Sigerson game in Belfast against St Mary's, who were fancied to win the thing. They had Tyrone guys like Stephen O'Neill, Mark Harte and Ciaran Gourley. I marked O'Neill and did very well. We managed to beat them 2–8 to 0–12 and we were absolutely buzzing on the way home.

We were coming down on the bus having a few cans, and suddenly, Wooly hops into the seat next to me. We were all agreed we were going to head to the Roost to celebrate our big win. That was the place to be, our friends would be there and it was always hopping.

But Wooly says, 'Why don't we go to the Students' Union and we'll work our way down then afterwards.'

I said, 'Are you joking, Wooly, there'll be nothing going on in the Students' Union. Everyone's down the Roost. We'll go straight there.'

'There's something good happening above in the Students' Union,' he said.

I said, 'Wooly, how about this – we'll go to the LA, the Leinster Arms, and start there.'

No dice. 'Okay,' I reasoned, 'how about Brady's?'

'The Students' Union is the place to be. I'm telling you,' he said. 'Let's go up there for a pint.'

'I'm not going up to the Students' Union. It's just too far up and we'll all have to get taxis and will get separated.'

Then he low-key says to me, 'I'm going to the SU. I'm barred from all the other bars.' I was in tears laughing when he said this.

He was a great teammate but, as Mick O'Dwyer (Micko) would say, a complete rogue.

Later, after my dad passed away, I finished the course and went on to Trinity.

From sitting in that lecturer's office in CIT to going in the gates of Trinity, I'm sure he would have been proud. Like a lot of his generation, maybe he didn't get the benefit of a top-level education and was just so committed to us getting the best for ourselves and our futures. He knew how important education was.

But the older we got, the more he let us make our own way too; he mellowed. We did too. It's a shame that we didn't have more years with him after that and get to enjoy each other's company more as adults.

*

The boys won a West Kerry championship against Annascaul in the early 1990s. Like a lot of local competitions, it means a huge amount and is notorious for being as rough as anything.

We hadn't won in ages and were in the wilderness for years until 1991. It was a bit like Manchester United when they won the Premier League in 1993 – a massive break-through after years of heartbreak. It gave us a glimpse of what could be possible and made me, as a kid, want to contribute to helping the club even more.

A few years later, in 1997, there was this huge piss-up the night we won another West Kerry title; I was still in school but Tomás was studying in Mary I.

My dad got Tomás – and Rob Mac Gearailt – out of the pub and put him at the bus stop in Dingle to head back to Limerick. It was a big win but keeping an eye on the books was the main thing with my father. After leaving the lads off, my dad headed back to Kane's in Ballyferriter for a pint but before he could even order, he saw Tomás and Rob on the other side of the bar sinking pints. In all the gin joints, in all the towns …

He put them both in the car and drove them to Limerick in silence.

I pulled a similar trick a couple of years later when we got to the county final in 2000, losing to Dr Crokes in Austin Stack Park, which is right next to the train station. My dad had learned his lesson this time and made sure I got on the train to head back to college.

But there wasn't a hope. I was sitting there thinking to myself, *Why should I miss out on the fun?* I hopped off again as the whistle went, ducked out of the station and met the boys in the Meadowlands Hotel in Tralee. I couldn't go home, of course, so stayed over in Páidí's homeplace – a safehouse on such occasions – and the next morning as I was sneaking out to start the long journey back up to Maynooth, I had to duck and dive past my dad as he crossed the yard.

He had his hands full with us. He was a mighty man.

Stick around with Páidí and you'd end up in some interesting company. People generally knew him as a charismatic, engaging personality, of course, but like all of us, he was deeper than the public perception.

He loved where he came from in west Kerry but found the winters bleak and often headed to Dublin to break up a week. He was like a minister for state being driven up by someone – on the phone in the passenger seat all the way up, calling his buddies around the country.

He really enjoyed the capital and had many friends around the city and would arrange some bit of business to be done or would attend some Fáilte Ireland meeting. He was on the board for many years, and I think he brought a lot of knowledge to the table as well as the perspective of someone running a small, independent business outside of Dublin.

Living out the road in Maynooth during those couple of college years, I got the benefit of his excursions several times. He'd ring me as he was heading up the road some days as I was attempting to study or get an assignment done.

'What are you up to?' he'd ask.

'Era, nothing major.'

'I'm coming into the city there,' he'd say. 'Come in and meet me.'

You couldn't refuse him. I'd snap the books shut and fling them into a corner and make a beeline for the train station.

One time I turned up to discover we were meeting Brian Cowen, who was minister for finance at the time – and would go on to be Taoiseach.

Páidí was interested in and became knowledgeable about politics and loved visiting Leinster House. He'd stop to admire framed portraits of Michael Collins and Cathal Brugha and the framed Proclamation from 1916. Back in Ard an Bhóthair, Charlie Haughey's face is dotted around the walls. His loyalties were never in question and he was staunchly Fianna Fáil.

Maybe it could have been different. Garret FitzGerald once told Mícheál Ó Muircheartaigh that when his parents returned from London, having met in the Gaelic League, their first Irish home was the coastguard station in Ventry. Perhaps Páidí would have ended up in Fine Gael if the FitzGeralds had stayed, Mícheál mused.

Páidí first met future Taoiseach Brian Cowen as a young law student from Clara in Co. Offaly. He had called into Kildare Street to meet his father, Ber, the Fianna Fáil TD for Laois–Offaly and their friendship endured.

We were having food in Wong's in Ranelagh and Cowen asked me what I was doing in college? I told him I was studying history and he asked what type. I told him about my modules on Irish and American history and he started peppering me with questions about the US Civil War or battles during the American War of Independence and he had a great knowledge.

After the meal, Cowen had to go and Páidí waved away his offers to pay telling him he'd take care of the bill.

Just then, Eamon Dunphy walked in the door.

Us two lads had nothing on, and Páidí said to Dunphy, 'Sit down there, Eamon, and join us.' I'd grown up watching him on TV, being such a charismatic and entertaining pundit on RTÉ's soccer coverage and it was a thrill to get to spend some time chatting to him.

He sat down and we had a great chat about Manchester United and politics, and I nodded along as the two older men debated various issues, sipping my free drink.

After some time, Dunphy excused himself, said his good-byes and went out the door.

As we were wondering where the night could take us, the famous golfer, Christy O'Connor Jr walked through the door.

Páidí, who seemed to know everyone, gave him a big welcome and pulled O'Connor Jr into our orbit. We passed another very enjoyable hour, with me eavesdropping on great stories about Jack Nicklaus and epic Irish Opens.

The restaurant staff were nearly sweeping up the floor around us and pulling down the shutters, when a waiter presented us with a bill that looked taller than Páidí after our long evening in the restaurant.

Christy, a real gentleman, said, 'Páidí, we had a great conversation, you have a long road home, let me pay for this.'

'Right you are, Christy,' Páidí said quickly as he threw my coat on my back and pushed me out the door. 'Thanks very much.' He was the ultimate rogue.

Charlie Haughey, as taoiseach, did a huge amount for west Kerry. All you need to do is drive into Dingle and look at the modern marina, which is so important, and the pier – that was all Charlie.

While he was a politician some people didn't like him, and his legacy is even more complicated now. But even though a lot of the country had strong, negative opinions about him, he was great to the fishermen of the area and Dingle people loved him.

He owned an island off the west Kerry coast – Inishvickallane – and he opened Páidí's pub in the 1980s.

They were complete opposites but had a strong friendship.

Every August, Charlie would start the regatta in Dingle and the fishermen brought him to the nicest fish restaurants in Dingle and they'd eat the best, freshest shellfish and drink the finest wine.

We played Cork in an All-Ireland semi-final in 2002. Páidí was manager, Darragh was captain and myself and Tomás were involved.

We got back to Dingle and basically gate-crashed this annual meal in The Half Door in the town, a beautiful restaurant that people will know. There were seven or eight fishermen, Páidí and Charlie – or as Páidí used to call him, whether he was in office or not, Taoiseach.

He was always Taoiseach to Páidí, no matter who came before him and after.

I was half embarrassed landing in the door of this nice restaurant but we were welcomed and told to sit down.

Jesus, there was food brought out – lobster, crab claws, prawns, lovely wine, the whole lot. This was just like seven-star stuff and was a change from some of the post-game grub we've had in various places around the country through the years.

Then, when the food was finished, Páidí said, with great ceremony, 'Would An Taoiseach and the fishermen like to join us back in Páidí's for a digestif?' A pint.

It was agreed that would be a good idea. We got back to Ventry and Páidí grabbed me by the elbow, 'Look, Marc, will you go behind the counter and pull the finest pint of porter for the Taoiseach, like a good lad.' I'd banked enough hours in the place down through the years and knew what I was doing.

'I will so,' I said and I went in behind the bar and made sure the pint was Guinness-advert perfect.

Not keen on spilling the stout over our guest of honour, I was careful carrying it over and placed the glass down slowly in front of him. I followed Páidí's lead in addressing him, 'There you go, Taoiseach.'

Páidí was watching this scene, half smiling, and he says suddenly, 'Oh Jesus Christ, would you look at the pint he's after putting up in front of our Taoiseach! For fuck sake, Marc.'

Páidí grabbed the pint, stormed away, leaving me totally embarrassed in front of Haughey and the entourage. I was also completely baffled; there was nothing wrong with the pint at all.

I followed Páidí in behind the bar, out of sight, where he took a nice slug out of the one I'd poured. He then grabbed the first pint that was sitting on the tray next to the taps and rushed back to the table.

'Now, Taoiseach,' he said, 'there's a proper pint for you.'

A few years later, we met again. It was the Saturday morning after an All Stars banquet and myself and Tomás were at a loose end when Páidí rang and enquired what we were up to.

I said, 'We're just here in the Burlington.'

'I'll have somebody outside in two minutes and we'll be gone off,' he said.

We weren't feeling too fresh but before we knew it, we were wending our way out to north Co. Dublin and jeez, I couldn't believe it when this fella with the look of a plain clothes garda waved us into Kinsealy, Haughey's well-known mansion.

It's part of my job now, but I've always had an interest in history, as well as current affairs and politics, and the impressive façade of the stately house was familiar from news broadcasts and footage of Charlie hopping into the back of his state car on the evening news throughout the 1980s and early 1990s. But here we were, hungover and in jeans.

We were welcomed in and I was struck by all these pictures of all these leaders down through the years: 1916 martyrs, European presidents, these great Irish political people who had changed Ireland, like Charlie's father-in-law, Seán Lemass.

Our host gave us a cup of tea in a lounge area and myself and Tomás were minding our Ps and Qs when Páidí said, 'You wouldn't have anything stronger, Taoiseach?' We got a bottle of beer, which I sipped politely, while the two men talked.

Páidí literally opened doors. Another night, while still a student, I ended up in the Four Seasons with him and was led into a room to be met by the businessman Denis O'Brien and Charlie's right-hand man P.J. Mara.

It was frightening. I thought I'd be better off out in Maynooth at the traffic-light party in the town or the Beat the Clock promotion in the Students' Union. But Páidí was comfortable in the company of these people and they enjoyed and respected him.

At one stage, Mara, still in a sharp pin-striped suit enquired if Darragh would run for Fianna Fáil in an upcoming election.

'I told you before P.J.,' Páidí said. 'I will deliver that one, kiddo.'

I was sat next to Páidí and I whispered, 'What are you talking about?'

'Shut up, you,' he says. But he just told him what they wanted to hear and he was well able. And they loved when Páidí told one of his stories – he'd have these fellas in tears laughing and he was the centre of attention at this table with some of the most important people in Ireland at the time.

We ended up in Renard's in the end and I got back to the books the following day.

CHAPTER 7

PÁIDÍ TIME

Colm Cooper tells a story of a helicopter carrying Páidí landing on a pitch in Killarney, causing a game to be stopped. An embarrassed Gooch was told to hop in and they went off to a golf event for a day of rubbing shoulders with the great and the good.

One time, I found myself on a private plane with him heading to a charity event in Manchester. Alex Ferguson's wife had organised a charity event and we were invited, through the kindness of a friend of Páidí's, Tom Bailey.

Of course, this was hugely exciting and we crammed into this private aircraft in our tuxedos. We were only up in the air and Páidí reached into his pocket – and then searched the others.

'Jesus Christ,' he said, 'Máire didn't put the dickie bow into the pocket at all.' Then he started.

'Tomás, give me your dickie bow there like a good lad.'

He obviously told him where to go.

'Marc, come here, I need a dickie bow, in fairness.'

This went on until we got to Old Trafford, where Páidí arrived open-collared. As we went in, I noticed this big bulge in his pocket. What does he have planned here? Eventually, Alex Ferguson – who was working the room – approached us.

'Alex, Páidí Ó Sé, Kerry manager,' he said, as he shook Fergie's hand. Then Páidí whipped his autobiography out of his pocket and pressed it into Fergie's hands.

'Give that a read, Alex,' he said. 'You might learn a few things.'

I had glandular fever once and Páidí sent me to the Meath legend, Seán Boylan, for a herbal treatment. While I was there, Seán said to me, 'You have an advantage over the whole country. Below there, you guys breathe that sea air every day. And you can't beat it. You can get into the water as much as you can.'

It's something that I never took for granted afterwards, having that luxury, because there are people that live in the Midlands or whatever, surrounded by bog or drumlins or whatever it may be, and they don't have the same facilities that we have.

Páidí understood the healing power of the seawater during his playing days.

He often advocated for people to take advantage of where

we came from. He had that sense of trusting himself, he trusted his instincts, trusted that he was doing the right thing and he was a good man to figure out if you were going well or not and was able to read that quickly in body language. People had one impression of him sometimes, but he was emotionally intelligent.

Maybe he got some of that reading of a player from Mick O'Dwyer too, but that's something that you either have or you don't – an understanding of people, whether they walk in the pub door or the stadium gate.

Páidí started secondary school in Dingle, but he pestered my grandparents to leave him go to the Sem – St Brendan's in Killarney. Of course, this was not because of any great academic ambitions, but rather so he could join an All-Ireland winning side. St Brendan's won the Hogan Cup in 1969.

It's said his parents thought the place might suit him – the carrot of the football might work better than any stick when it came to motivating him to crack open a book.

He settled in quickly as a boarder and after a year in the building was training with the senior team. Ultimately, he won two Munster College titles and in his first of many games at Croke Park, lined out in the 1972 All-Ireland final. But St Patrick's made sure Páidí's first outing on Jones' Road would be a losing one.

He was less amenable to work in the classroom. Páidí showed throughout his life – despite people underestimating him – just how intelligent he was in different ways.

He was a great businessman, the sharpest marketing mind this side of Madison Avenue, and proved as a player and, mostly, as a manager how emotionally intelligent he was.

He could motivate, lead, read someone's mood, understand what drove them. He was ahead of his time when it came to video analysis and strength and conditioning and – a valuable asset as a publican – he was quick-witted.

But as a pupil – and perhaps throughout his life – his attention span was short, and he'd often want to move on to a new subject or task.

I know as a teacher, nowadays students have more support and there's more understanding of how each student is wired. But in a classroom in Kerry in the 1970s, such allowances weren't offered to pupils who failed immediately to slot into the traditional teaching methods.

His time in the Sem came to a sudden end in 1973 when he was 17 – he later alluded to illicit material found in his locker. 'Contraband, Marc,' he'd say with a shake of his head. It was a blow that must have been tough for a young lad to bounce back from. He was off to Listowel.

The connection with Listowel was there because my mom and dad lived in the town.

First my father rented a house with Bob Sullivan, a friend from Dingle, and they enjoyed life in the town as young men. Later my mom and dad moved to north Kerry for my father's work as an agricultural officer and Fergal, Darragh and Tomás were born in Listowel.

And, as it happened, they ended up with Páidí there too. After he was kicked out of the Sem my grandmother said, 'Right, you're moving in with Michael and Joan in Listowel.'

One of the little, unexpected treats in my life is when someone approaches me to tell me a Páidí story I haven't heard before. There's a good book about the golfer Phil Mickelson – a multi-dimensional character, let's say. For the first chapter the author Alan Shipnuck asked other golfers, caddies, friends for *their* Phil story. Everyone had one.

It seems to be the same with Páidí.

I had a parent–teacher meeting a couple of years back and I was chatting to this lady about her son. And as I was finishing up by complimenting her son's behaviour and work ethic, she interrupted, 'Sorry, do you mind if I tell you a quick story?'

'You don't know me really,' she said, 'but my auntie was a nun in Listowel and she was a teacher. When she came to the school she was asked to give Páidí grinds in geography.'

Páidí was training with the school on Mondays,

Wednesdays and Fridays – but on Tuesdays and Thursdays, he'd go get the grinds after the school day. Around this time too, he developed the habit of taking a pint as well.

And so, on a Tuesday he'd have a couple of pints in Mike the Pies on the way home from the grinds. And this nun was in on the scheme and Páidí had her sworn to secrecy. When Beatrice rang twice a week asking how the geography grinds were going, she'd say, 'Oh, he's fine; he's a great student.'

Perhaps she was saying a prayer for him and his exams too. Just when you think you've heard all the yarns. It just shows the charisma and roguery of the man, even at that age. He could persuade a nun to lie to his parents, so he could get out for a couple of pints every Tuesday.

He was loved in Listowel.

The school had never won a thing until Páidí came when they got to the O'Sullivan Cup final where, inevitably, they came up against his old school, the Sem – the aristocrats of Kerry college football.

It went to a replay and then extra time but Páidí scored 2–2 against his alma mater to pull off a huge upset. The Sem had Pat Spillane and a typically excellent team, but Páidí had driven on his new school to an incredible win.

The family moved back west around the time I was born. But we always kept the Listowel connection.

We never went to Spain or Portugal or any of those

places for a break in the summer – that's when my mom was working hardest. Instead, it was always up to Ballybunion or some place. It gave my dad a chance to meet all his cronies and friends in north Kerry. So that link was important when Listowel came calling with me last year asking would I get involved?

My wife, Ellen, and I have a young family, I've a busy job and it's a huge commitment throwing your lot in with a team, but I liked the fact that there was an authentic connection. Another couple of clubs had enquired about me joining up, but then when Listowel came, I just knew it was the right decision. There was a bit of meaning to it.

As importantly, they had footballers and we went on a right run. There was a good team there but the cliché about a 'sleeping giant' suited well. We got to the junior premier county final and managed to beat Ballymacelligott after extra time. What a thrill.

And then to celebrate it with the lads in Christy Welch's Bar in Listowel all that night was special. There were people coming up to me, telling me stories about my parents. I learned my mother was on the committee for the soccer during her time there; there was never soccer in west Kerry but there was in Listowel. I heard tales about my dad as a young man. It was lovely to hear all those yarns.

We won a Munster title next and got to the All-Ireland club final against Arva of Cavan in the end. I'm friends with Hugh Hourican in the Boar's Head on Capel Street for many years now. He's a proud Arva man and we stayed away from each other in the run up.

They were a serious team and we came up short. But to be part of a Listowel group getting to Croke Park was a gift. I've no doubt that my dad would be proud of that.

CHAPTER 8

THE FIELD

I live in Tralee now; that's where my own family are but me and Ellen often talk, when driving back west, how great it would be if we could get back here full time at some stage.

I know how lucky I was to grow up here, between the mountains and the sea. My brother Fergal built a house back maybe a hundred yards from the crossroads.

He was the one, growing up, who showed the most interest in farming and he's still the one at it today. My mother's side had a farm, of course, and we grew up there. I have great memories of saving the hay, up on tractors at the age of nine or ten.

I often remember one summer in particular when the weather was incredible and the fun we had bringing the bales into the barn, stacking them in the barn and jumping off like we were going off the top rope at WrestleMania.

I recall being up in this tractor, a Massey Ferguson 165 or 135 owned by a local farmer, Seánie Moriarty, who's passed away now. Seánie would hitch a big trailer onto this tractor and there must have been 120 bales piled up on this thing, and me swaying and Tomás on top of it all. They talk about health and safety.

If it split it would be game over – you'd end up three fields over.

We had a small farm at home as well ourselves, a 20- or 30-acre holding. My dad, the agricultural officer, had two cows and dry cattle and we had a good few sheep. Often people would say to us at Ard an Bhóthair, 'Sure, what would you know about farming?' And little would they realise that we did a small bit of farming ourselves as well.

We were on the sustainability trend before it was cool. My mom had cabbage, carrots, tomatoes; my dad had the potatoes and we'd have a big day then when you were digging up all the spuds and we'd carry them into the shed.

As kids, we didn't get paid for any of this work – it was our own hay that we were saving for the cattle, our own food for the dinner table that we were harvesting, and I was grateful because, during the summer, it was a day you'd look forward to.

There was a river between the bit of land we had so then the tractor and trailer would have to pick up all the bales, and we'd have to manoeuvre to go through the river and come out the other side. For us as kids, it was the best craic of all time trying to get this machine through the water.

We were nearly hoping that the whole thing would go over for the comedy of it. Then we'd bring in the bales and if I was up on the top, I'd be trying to fire them down on top of Tomás and hit him on top of the head – or vice versa. There was nothing funnier to me.

Even during the wintertime, my dad would give us chores to do like give the animals the hay or the feed or clean out sheds. But he was not a big farmer, by any stretch. He'd often have other things that he'd have to do – like his day job – and he'd have to neglect the farm. But we loved what little we had as a family all the same.

We didn't have tractors or trailers – they'd always be hired in. But then we used to go over to my uncle Mike's farm.

He was Michael Kavanagh, my mom's brother, and he had a plant hire and you can imagine how attractive it was for a young lad: he had every machine known to man. Diggers, JCBs, dumpers – and his farm as well, full of tractors and trailers. This fella was the real deal and his place was like Disneyland to us.

The thrill we'd get when we were let drive tractors or JCBs was amazing. In later years he bought a quarry outside Lispole and there were times when you'd have to blast the stone with dynamite. There'd be detectives there because it was the time of the Troubles and dynamite was a valuable commodity.

Then when you'd blast the dynamite, you'd have to be gone outside a mile radius. My God, the anticipation and fun waiting for the blast! I really got on great with Uncle Mike, as we used to call him, and he'd bring you everywhere and anywhere like agriculture shows, fat stock sales, the ploughing.

I don't think any of us ever really thought of making a living off the farm. There were four of us brothers and there wouldn't have been enough land to farm and it wasn't something that I would have had enough passion for anyway.

The only one of the four of us who had the enthusiasm for it was my eldest brother, Fergal, and my uncle Mike identified the interest and nourished it. He bought a pure-bred sheep for Fergal – which would have been expensive – and ever since then, Fergal has bred these Texel sheep.

He looks after them better than he looks after himself and he's won lots of prizes – or the rams have, at least. Fergal's house now is only a kick of the ball away from our homeplace and if you go back there in the lead-up to a competition you'll see his two boys, Niall and Conall, and his daughter, Niamh, cleaning the sheep. Fergal would be shampooing the wool and brushing them.

And I swear to God, the sheep would be cleaner than Fergal himself. There was one year around Christmastime, one of the sheep he was feeding for a good while sadly died suddenly. They're temperamental enough animals that can drop like anything and this poor divil died, leaving Fergal heartbroken.

It wasn't a source of amusement at all, seeing an animal die, but just watching how it affected Fergal, had the rest of us telling him to get a life. 'Would you get a life for yourself?'

So, if any of us got the bug for the farming, it's him.

Lambing season is a major event in his house. He's a principal of a school now and around February time he must keep a close eye on the sheep at home too. He has cameras throughout the place like it's Fort Knox. No matter where he is he can check on what's happening on his phone.

And he has some help. Micí Ó Conchúir – or Sticky Mickey, as he's better known in our club because of his man-marking capabilities in his playing days – is part of a neighbourhood watch unit that can help if needed and the two of them could be up all hours of the night looking after an animal that's about to lamb.

Dara Ó Cinnéide asked Fergal a couple of years back if he would be manager of An Ghaeltacht. He'd successfully coached An Ghaeltacht for the large part of 10 years from 1996 up to 2005 or so. But Fergal said, 'Sure, what about the sheep?'

Cinnéide was like, 'Jesus, we'll help you. We'll take care of it.'

So, the club is in the farming business now too.

*

But farming was something we all experienced growing up, along with football and the music and life in west Kerry. I think growing up where we did, we all took something from it and saw the beauty in it. It's in our blood.

As I've said, my mom was born near Lispole. The home-place is a cowhouse now. It's on the route of the Kerry Camino, from Tralee to Dingle. I was walking the road one morning with a group of Transition Year students and we passed the old homestead. I said to the lads, 'You see that cowhouse, boys – my mother was born inside there.'

They thought I was having them on. But when you see the farm that was there and that they left, I realise how it rubbed off on us. There's no doubt about that.

You might think the football gene was inherited from my father's side of the family but Uncle Mike, my mother's brother, was always quick to tell us that he lined out in Croke Park. He was playing an instrument for the Ventry band on the field before a game.

My mom's family weren't particularly sporty, even though my mom ran the Dublin City Marathon and was fit out back in the day. I think when we started playing seriously, Mikey took an interest in it and always kept track of the scores and how we were doing.

I've given them all away now more or less, but I always had a love of jerseys and loved collecting them as I grew up and throughout my playing days. I had nearly every jersey of every county as a kid – and a lot of them had been bought by Uncle Mike.

He was a completely different uncle to Páidí and Tom on the other side, but my God, did I love spending time with him. He'd pick me up at home in his beautiful Isuzu Trooper and take me to some land he had around Ventry overlooking the water. And he'd leave me drive down back towards the beach.

He worked hard and he did well for himself but he died young, suffering a brain haemorrhage. He had those kidney issues which afflicted that side of the family. He was on dialysis for years and eventually got a kidney transplant. In the end he dropped dead at 54 in 2004 while in Scotland with his youngest daughter, Della. It was a huge shock to us but he was a great uncle and his wife Marion is my godmother.

CHAPTER 9

HERE YOU COME AGAIN

The pub became a powerful focal point in west Kerry and we were lucky to meet so many interesting people, from all walks of life.

There's a great photograph of myself and Tomás with Michael O'Hehir, who's an elderly man at the time and he's inside in the wheelchair that people would have seen him in when he was brought out before the 1988 All-Ireland football final, having been absent from the airwaves.

His voice and mind were a connection to all those All-Ireland finals we'd grown up rewinding and rewatching, and it was a thrill to meet him.

Jack Lynch came through the doors, and it was explained that this man had won six All-Irelands with Cork – five in hurling and one in football. And Páidí would add as a footnote that he was taoiseach twice.

There's a picture above the bar of me and my old friend Tom Cruise. Maverick and Goose.

Far and Away was being filmed in west Kerry and half the peninsula was involved in some way or another.

Páidí got wind that an A-lister was around the place, so he made it his mission to get him on a stool inside in the bar – and one day he managed it.

Tom Long's brother Mike was the Del Boy of the parish. If Tom was squeaky clean, Mike Long was a different proposition – a great character and hugely appreciated personality around the place. A local farmer, they used to call him the boyeen.

Cruise came in with his entourage and Mike Long was straight over to him, 'Well Tom, you wouldn't buy a round for a local peasant farmer?' he said.

Cruise took it all in his stride. Páidí – never one to miss a trick – had photographers organised.

There's a huge photograph from behind the counter with Cruise and my grandmother and the 1984 Centenary Cup which was supposed to go back up to Dublin in 1985. It's still behind the bar now.

Páidí, who was captain, said, 'Over my dead body is that trophy going back up there.'

I was too young to witness the visit of Dolly Parton. I'm often reminded that I was in bed that night, still a young fella.

Imagine it. One of the best-known singers in the world popped in on an impromptu visit while she was on holidays in the area.

Páidí presented her with his jersey from the 1985 All-Ireland. When he quipped it hadn't been washed since, Dolly said, 'I was hoping there was still sweat on it.' Later she took to the stage, performing her heartfelt song 'Coat of Many Colours' for the delighted patrons. You can see my old friend Steve Cooney by her side, accompanying her.

We often wondered what happened to the jersey and did she have any *meas* on this memento. Dolly went on *Liveline* some years later and revealed that she still has the Kerry jersey hanging in her home, a cherished souvenir of her visit to the pub.

After Tom Cruise visited, Páidí often referred to his friend and let on that they were still in contact.

When *The West Wing* and *Apocalypse Now* star Martin Sheen landed in Ventry, he had a chance to add another A-lister name to his rolodex. But Páidí wasn't a man for a boxset of *The West Wing*.

'Who's Martin Sheen?' says Páidí.

We told him, 'A big Hollywood actor.' His demeanour changed immediately.

'Martin, how are you?! Welcome to Ard an Bhóthair!'

Ever the host, Páidí offered his VIP guest a pint. Sheen,

famously a recovering alcoholic, replied that he didn't drink any more.

Páidí contemplated this, paused at the tap and replied, 'Era Christ, you'll have one?'

Sheen was sound though and chatted away for the guts of an hour. He was interested in the various pictures on the wall and was good company. When he eventually left, we blackguarded Páidí by suggesting he rush out and tell Sheen to pass on his regards to his friends in Hollywood.

He tore out the door and roared, 'Martin! Martin!' until Sheen rolled down the window like Wilson Pickett at the end of *The Commitments*. 'Say hello to Tom for me will you.'

Weeks later, he produced a folded-up letter, in suspiciously familiar handwriting, that was purportedly from Sheen, thanking Páidí for his hospitality. It contained the detail that Tom Cruise sent his regards. We'll never know now.

There is a picture above the bar of another celebrity encounter, between Páidí and Gregory Peck.

Some of the Kerry panel were in the US in the 1990s. In Los Angeles, a group of the West Kerry representatives – Darragh, Páidí, and Fintan Ashe from Dingle – met with Fr James Kavanagh.

A Ventry man, he was working as a curate in the parish that included Beverly Hills. His congregation was made up of some of the biggest names in Hollywood, including Peck.

After the priest gave the appreciative group a tour of LA, he asked if they'd like to meet Peck, who was a mass goer and someone Fr James knew well.

Páidí shrugged his shoulders: 'Grand.'

Peck greeted the group at the doors of his sprawling mansion and they spoke of his family connections to Ireland, his time filming *Moby Dick* in Youghal and he showed the group into a room containing his awards and some memorabilia.

Páidí interrupted Peck reciting a monologue from *Moby Dick* to ask the host for a bottle of beer, as he said he was thirsty.

After Peck, who was then an old man, excused himself for a nap – the group looked around at the movie paraphernalia.

'Would you like a photo with one of the Oscars,' Darragh says he asked Páidí.

'I'm grand,' he said, 'sure, haven't I the All Stars at home?'

Unless you were a Hollywood star, Páidí's was always a good place to hide out back west.

A neighbour of ours, Mick Galwey, the former Ireland rugby international, would have known this well when he and the Munster lads needed to retreat after a particular defeat to their big rivals.

It was around the time that Leinster were taking over after Munster's early domination of the nascent professional game here. They beat Munster in Croke Park in a big European game – while the Aviva was being developed.

Galwey, who built a summer home at Ard an Bhóthair, picked up the bat phone and called for help.

'Páidí, listen, I have the Munster guys here and we need somewhere to bolt up and have a quiet few pints, maybe tell a few home truths and get the show back on the road. Is there any chance we can come down and get the Munster lads in. You can get a few of the locals, the fellas that are into the rugby, but obviously keep it quiet.' That was the gist.

No bother at all, said Páidí, 'I'll fucking sort it all,' he says. The next day, the Munster delegation hit as far as Lispole and there's this huge sign on the side of the road: 'Páidí Ó Sé's: The Munster Rugby team will be in tonight. All welcome.'

They came through Lispole, another huge sign hammered into the ditch: 'Come meet the Munster Rugby team in Páidí Ó Sé's.'

Oh my God. Galwey's stress levels are rising in the bus, surrounded by the likes of O'Gara, Howlett and Quinlan. They get as far as Dingle: two more freshly produced signs, before they get on the road back to Ventry.

Now, the pub has a big car park; there's usually loads of space. But as the bus pulls into Ard an Bhóthair they see there are cars jammed in everywhere and abandoned on the side of the road like it's a county final day.

Galwey comes in and he says, 'Páidí, what the fuck? I told you to keep things quiet. Jesus Christ, man, these fellas just want to drown their sorrows.'

Páidí puts his hand on Galwey's shoulder and says, 'Mick, I knew from your voice that all they needed was a gee-up and these fellas will give it to them.'

CHAPTER 10

AN GHAELTACHT

The feeling I always had of being from An Ghaeltacht was that we were the underdogs, the lads from back west, the unknowns. It suited us.

To start to understand the club and where this feeling came from, it's useful first to get a sense of the geography and the scale of the place. It's a huge area that draws young kids in from all over the peninsula.

People will be familiar with the region, which now attracts visitors throughout the year. Anything west of Dingle is ours. It's beautiful terrain, made up of mountains and coastline, that I find I appreciate even more as I get older.

Behind our homeplace is Mount Eagle, next to that is Cruach Mhárthain. The road between the two mountains is An Clasach, which leads you down into Dunquin. With the Atlantic behind you, climb high and you're rewarded with a view of the Blasket Islands.

Westwards, is Inis Tuaisceart – An Fear Marbh or the Dead Man. On a clear day you can make out Inishvickallane, the island Charlie Haughey made his home. Look eastward and you take in the horseshoe of Ventry and Dingle Bay beyond it.

Though a wild and vast corner of the country, it's sparsely populated and has been affected by emigration for centuries. There are a few parishes within the area like ours: Ard an Bhóthair. There's Dunquin where Kruger's pub is, as well as Ballyferriter, Ballydavid and Feothanach, at the foot of Mount Brandon where Dara Ó Cinnéide is from.

We grew up as clubmates and great friends but, to give you an idea of the scale of the land that An Ghaeltacht encapsulates, it would take 25 minutes to drive to Ó Cinnéide's homeplace from ours.

Because of that distance between the parishes and schools, we didn't know the likes of Dara at all well when we were young, apart from my brother Darragh – they played underage together.

We were all in different primary schools, which fed into our club – Cill Mhic an Domhnaigh, where we went; as well as An Feothanach, An Mhuiríoch, Glens, Dún Chaoin, Ventry and Ballyferriter.

I'm not sure if it's unique to our club, but it was unusual that us club players didn't know each other at all when we got going. Liam Ó Rócháin, Tommy Dowd, Seán Ó Catháin and Jack Griffin were the mentors at underage. As the youngest, I was watching all this, looking at the lads playing and wanting all the time to be part of it.

When we were growing up, we had a primary schools competition that was as important as the Sam Maguire to us: the Corn Mhic Eoin.

It was the first time we encountered the lads who would become our clubmates, and it was fiercely competitive. The kingpins, the Real Madrids of the peninsula, were Feothanach, around 12 or 13 miles from our homeplace and where my brother Fergal is now principal.

That competition – from 8 years old to about 12 – was our first introduction to football.

My first year, Feothanach emerged with this tall, athletic full forward who was highly effective. Dáithí Ó Sé, who went on to be a TV presenter and, more importantly, the Rose of Tralee host, was a decent footballer back then.

Those lads won the cup year after year after year. But my last year playing, we won it at last. We won the Corn Mhic Eoin, our All-Ireland. For the record, Tomás never won one, which is a card I'm sometimes forced to play.

The stories and names that thread together the club's history were passed on to us. We learned of the feats of men like Batt Garvey, our cousin Tom Long, our neighbour Mícheál Ó Sé and many more.

Us brothers lapped up those tales and Páidí was a jukebox

for stories; he had an authentic passion for that legacy. We tried to add to the club's story. Fergal led the way, as usual for us, and started off playing with An Ghaeltacht.

Darragh and Dara Ó Cinnéide's team came behind Fergal's group and really started to make an impression. The heavyweights of Kerry football from the big towns – Austin Stacks, Laune Rangers, Dr Crokes – had years of a winning tradition, carving up the big competitions between them each year. With this exciting young team coming through, our club set about trying to change that pattern.

Embroidered on our shirts is the club motto: *Sprid, Croí, Caid, Teanga.*

It translates as: Spirit, Heart, Football, Language.

Traditionally, *caid* was the rough and ready game played between villages or parishes around the country before someone thought to write down the rules of football. Groups of men would try to get a ball over a line that was chalked out between the factions. In the Kerry Gaeltacht, we'd still call football '*caid*' now. I'm not sure what that tells you about how we approach the game.

And *teanga*? The Irish language is central to our identity in west Kerry – and it's the same in the GAA club. We were proud of being different. Proud of our culture. It can also be an advantage.

As well as the familiar wind whipping in off the Atlantic and the sandy Gallarus pitch, teams were often left disconcerted by our shouted communications *as Gaeilge*. Once in a game against Austin Stacks in Tralee, I was marking my old friend, Kieran Donaghy – I was full back, he was full forward. I was talking to the young corner back next to me, *as Gaeilge*, and instructing him on a few things.

Donaghy, standing next to me, looking to the sky, said, 'Jesus Christ, why didn't I just listen to my Irish teacher in school?'

The huge thing with An Ghaeltacht was playing in the Comórtas Peile na Gaeltachta, where all the Irish teams in the country meet. It's an All-Ireland for Gaeltacht teams, attracting sides from Galway, Donegal, Cork and beyond, and my God, they were fierce contests and so hard to win.

We went down to Baile Bhuirne in Cork one time, playing Naomh Abán. They had a team featuring Anthony Lynch and Micheál Cronin – big Cork players.

We had almost a full-strength side too and the game was a draw at full time and a draw after extra time before they beat us by a point after a second period of extra time.

It was a great contest and I remember Micheál Cronin's father coming out onto the pitch and he summed it up, '*Epic a bhí ann* [It was epic].'

They are great games, only enriched by the shared language.

Darragh made a full-blooded tackle and somebody was roaring *as Gaeilge*, 'Put him off, put him off!' Somebody else in the crowd wondered, '*Cé hé* [Who]?' The reply was, '*An savage mór*' [The big savage].' We used that one afterwards once or twice.

Another year at the Comórtas, we played Cill na Martra, the team of the Cork great Noel O'Leary. I knew from years of experience what a tough competitor he was. During the course of the game, the ball broke between us and I knew immediately I was completely exposed. Bang – Noel took the opportunity to nail me and my ballooning ankle signalled the end of my tournament.

The following day, Tomás texted me to say Noel was looking for me and would he pass on my number. 'Yeah, of course.' The phone buzzed within minutes with an incoming call from an apologetic O'Leary.

An Ghaeltacht's pitch, Gallarus, is right in the middle of the peninsula.

Other teams didn't particularly like coming back there, despite the beautiful setting. It's a hard, sandy pitch – Páidí once said we should keep camels on it, not footballers. It's set out next to the beach and the wind is a 16th player.

Dara Ó Cinnéide took a free kick one day with the posts on his right. But he aimed it straight out towards New York, before the wind caught the ball and just pulled it back in and over the bar.

He was like a good skipper of a fishing boat, knowing the personality of every gust of wind that came in from the Atlantic. The opposition were just watching with their mouths open as the ball sailed over.

Cinnéide, a very bright guy, had high skill levels on the football pitch and he played Gallarus like an adept golfer on his home course. We'd often reflect at half time in a game at home, saying we're against the wind in the second half and we're only six or five up. That was never a bother to us, we nearly preferred playing against the wind than with the wind, because we just knew how to play with it back there.

We created a fortress out of Gallarus – nobody liked coming the hour from Killarney or the hour from Tralee and we very rarely got beaten back there. It's different now the way the football year is split into inter-county and club seasons, but in our day, the Kerry players were absent from the clubs a lot more.

And to give our fellas the greatest credit that they ever deserved, our team played most of the county league games without us. But they kept us up in Division One throughout that whole great decade, our golden era. We owed that to clubmen like J.J. Corduff, Cathal Ó Dubhda, Brendy Walsh, Micí Ó Conchúir, Riobard Mac Gearailt.

All these fellas were keeping us up at senior club Division One, which is tough in Kerry, and we were there for the guts of 10 years. We knew we'd clock back in after the inter-county season with the team and our season in good shape, thanks to their efforts.

*

My kids don't believe me, but as children we'd make our own way, the seven or eight miles, to training or matches in Gallarus on bicycles. We'd cycle in convoy up the hill and across the peninsula, train and head home again.

I was doing that until I was about 13 or 14 years of age. After that I could go with our neighbour Mícheál Ó Sé, who was the coach. We used to just cycle a mile up the road and he'd pick us up.

That whole commute was an education and a training. Hail, rain or snow, we were on our bikes. And that wasn't just our gang at Ard an Bhóthair, that was everyone. There were lads hopping on Raleigh Choppers and BMXs all over the peninsula and were committed to getting to Gallarus.

For better or worse, it's different times now, of course. There's a lot more traffic around the place for a start so it's less safe for young kids to negotiate the roads. You pass Gallarus now on a summer's evening and there are cars lined up outside on the ditch – everyone gets dropped there.

It's a class set up. You go in the gate and the main stand is on the far side of the pitch like a windbreaker, sheltering the field from the Atlantic.

A sign on the dressing room building reads: '*Is í an Ghaelainn ár dTeanga. Labhraimís í* [Irish is our language. Let's speak it].' Another tells visitors to '*Bain súp as an lá* [Make the most of the day]!' Good advice.

The beach is right behind the stand. A lot of summer

nights after a session on the pitch, we'd go down and throw ourselves into the water and come back up. It's amazing to have that opportunity. Sports scientists will explain the benefit of that fresh, salt water right after a tough evening's physical work. People pay money to get that.

When you pad back out of the water with your team-mates, you know too that's good for the head and the soul as well.

Sometimes – maybe most often – you can trace a club's transformation back to a person or two who had a vision and a passion. That was the case with An Ghaeltacht.

The underage structures in the club were poor. We weren't properly organised or getting the most out of the talent on the peninsula.

Liam Ó Rócháin was a teacher in Ballyferriter, and he got a handle on things. Nowadays there are several adults with each underage team. He came in and was training U12s, U14s, U16s and minors, on his own. It's hard to imagine. He basically lived in the club pitches in Gallarus, when he wasn't teaching. Talk about a busman's holiday.

Dara Ó Cinnéide and Darragh's team were good and would go on to make up the nucleus of An Ghaeltacht's side that got all the way to Croke Park.

Their age group won the U12 county final, then the Division One U14, the Division One U16 championship, next the Division One minor county final, beating the top teams like Stacks, Laune Rangers, all the aristocrats of Kerry football.

The word was out – An Ghaeltacht were coming.

Darragh's team graduated to adult football and West Kerry won the county final – mainly because of a nucleus that was coming from An Ghaeltacht. An Ghaeltacht had always been a novice club – never reaching senior. We nearly got up from intermediate in 1994 with a 19-year-old Darragh but missed out to Milltown in the final. But then pieces of the jigsaw started to be added.

Rob Mac Gearailt and Cathal Ó Dubhda came the year after Darragh and Dara Ó Cinnéide. We had senior players like Micí Ó Conchúir, who would have been playing with Páidí; J.J. Corduff and our own Fergal. Every year there were more players coming down the conveyor belt that the likes of Liam had set rolling: Tomás Ó Concubhar; the next year, Aodán Mac Gearailt; Tomás who was playing in All-Ireland minor finals the following year in All-Ireland U21 finals.

A year later, I'm coming through and with one of my best friends, Eoin Ó Cruadhlaoich, as well as Conall Ó Cruadhlaoich – who played three years with the Kerry minors.

It was like the first reel of a good heist movie where the gang is being put together.

*

Everything we achieved afterwards can be traced back to 1991 and the West Kerry championship.

In Dingle, the West Kerry championship is played between An Ghaeltacht, Annascaul, Lispole, Castlegregory and Dingle. Lispole had a monopoly on the competition during Páidí's days, winning 13 on the trot.

We hadn't won a West Kerry championship in 20-something years. I watched on as an 11-year-old as An Ghaeltacht beat the kingpins Annascaul, with Fergal outstanding in midfield. The club went back a bit afterwards before Darragh's team started coming through.

In 1997 we won the West Kerry championship after a replay and extra time against Dingle. There were huge celebrations. These local competitions like the West Kerry championship and even going back as far as the Corn Mhic Eoin in primary school are important. I finished up with nine West Kerry medals and they're medals I'm very proud of.

In 1997, I was a teenager and a sub on the team. We were in Quinn's pub before the game, having our meeting, and Páidí came in. He had nothing to do with the team officially, but he'd been asked to give us a speech.

I remember the words and the way he got his message across to this day: discipline and ruthlessness were the themes. We were inside in the dressing room afterwards, preparing for the game, and we had lovely new Adidas gear with very smart red and white shorts.

Richie O'Mahony – a very important player for us who died sadly, very young, in 2024 – realised he had no shorts. I was instructed, as a young lad on the subs bench, to give Richie my nicks. I was absolutely gutted.

It's funny now but I was nearly in tears slowly taking off the shorts in the dressing room and handing them over to this man.

The following year we faced our fiercest rivals, Dingle. This is like Springfield and Shelbyville or the Yankees and Red Sox. It's a huge, intense, local rivalry.

We got to the 1998 intermediate final in Austin Stack Park in Tralee – so too did our neighbours. It's something that's happened to me a lot throughout my career where you're coming up against old foes in championship deciders for the first time.

In 2007 with Kerry, we came up against Cork in the All-Ireland final, the first time Kerry ever played Cork in the championship decider, and a lot of the talk by us was that you can't lose to your greatest rivals in *that* game.

This felt just as big in a way. We'd beaten them the year before but only after a replay and extra time.

The four of us brothers were on the team and Fergal was just so important. He played a few National League games in 1997 for Kerry and then, unfortunately, did his hamstring and he was gone for the rest of the season, effectively missing out on winning the All-Ireland.

But he took on the role of coach and oversaw An Ghaeltacht and got the team into tip-top shape.

We beat Dingle comfortably in the final, with Darragh just outstanding. I very nearly kicked a point from wing back but Diarmuid Murphy in goal – all 6 ft 4 of him – grabbed the ball from over the crossbar.

But what a day. We'd made it to the senior ranks at last. Winning that 1998 intermediate was massive for us – it felt like the start of something big.

CHAPTER 11

COME WEST ALONG THE ROAD

The perception is that Páidí wasn't much of a clubman in his playing days.

An Ghaeltacht weren't at the top table during his football career and he may well have focused his efforts on making sure he was right for inter-county.

But he was the fella who designed An Ghaeltacht's jersey. The club meant a lot to him.

He admitted himself that he was completely focused on Kerry as a player. That fixation was to the detriment of his career in the Garda Síochána, his own business later and, he said, his commitment to An Ghaeltacht.

After he retired though he returned to the club and took charge in the late 1980s when he opened his contacts book.

P.O. got on to Paddy O'Mahony, who owns the Meadowlands Hotel, near where I live now, in Tralee.

Paddy's from the Gaeltacht, still lives in the Gaeltacht, and he's a very successful businessman with a fish factory as well as the hotel. That call was the start of a long and happy sponsorship – every Ghaeltacht jersey I've ever pulled on since has had '*Iasc Ui Mhathuna* [O'Mahony's Fish]' emblazoned on it.

After a debate in the club about our colours, we ended up wearing red and green – rather than the red and white of my preference – in 1998/99.

That year we had our first ever senior game against the mighty South Kerry. This was the district of Mick O'Connell and Mick O'Dwyer and now featured Maurice Fitzgerald.

We went to their place and managed to earn a draw, meaning we'd have a replay.

The first senior game in Gallarus was a sell-out. The club installed fences and ferocious work was done to get the place ready.

People came from all over the county, and beyond, to be there. The people of the area really backed us that year.

I've never seen Gallarus packed like I saw it that day. It was amazing. You know the *D'Unbelievables* sketch with the two guards warning lads about abandoning cars on county final day? 'You can't do that!' Highly applicable.

I wasn't playing. I repeated my Leaving Cert and my father – always the one looking out for the books – said no football for the year.

By the time I rejoined the panel, I was playing catch-up trying to get back in and there were certainly no favours from my brother, Fergal, either. You, rightly, had to earn your spot and all I was at that stage was a former Kerry minor really.

We beat South Kerry after a replay, and Maurice Fitzgerald broke his leg in Gallarus, sadly. We went on to play the galacticos of East Kerry, who were going for three in a row and were an unbelievable team: Séamus Moynihan, Johnny Crowley, Donal Daly, Declan O'Keeffe – just a plethora of great players. We got destroyed. But we'd made a big step up.

A huge amount of work was put into the club throughout this time by plenty of people. Chief amongst them was Tom Crowley who had produced beautiful programmes for people in Gallarus that day.

Every club, I hope, has a gem or two like this man. He was originally from Waterford and the principal in Meánscoil na Toirbhirte in Dingle. He fulfilled various roles within the club throughout the years and was chairperson but was so vital behind the scenes.

Liam Ó Rócháin and Mícheál Ó Sé did so much and led the club but you also need somebody who's going to do all the other hard work, the grafting, whether it be raising money or liaising with Croke Park.

Tom did everything from drawing in sponsorship to drawing the markings on the pitch.

Another former taoiseach, Bertie Ahern, and his wife at the time, Miriam, and the two kids used to come down and stay with Tom's family in Ballyferriter. Tom's two sons, Eoin and Conall, were around my age as well and we were great friends growing up.

Importantly, Tom Ó Cruadhlaoich was also the man who gave my wife Ellen her first job in Meánscoil na Toirbhirte. He was very good to her and they became friendly. At that time, my commute brought me the opposite way and I'd pass this lady on the Conor Pass heading for Dingle, as I was wending towards Tralee.

It's funny the way things work. Myself and Ellen were in the Tuition Centre in Tralee, with a year between us, and later in Maynooth at the same time. Later again in Trinity we studied concurrently but never met.

When our paths did cross on the Conor Pass, I remember saying to myself, 'Jesus, who's this good-looking woman?' – though we wouldn't meet for some time after that.

When we won our first county final, Tom was in the background with a camera throughout and the pictures now are so cherished.

He had his own little office in his house downstairs and Eoin, who lives in Long Beach in California now, goes down into the den as they call it whenever he's home and goes through these photographs. My phone will light up, I'll open it and be transported back to a time and space thanks to a vivid team photograph.

Tom died suddenly a couple of years ago and like Páidí's and my father's deaths, it was a huge shock. He was a crucial part of the club's success and important in our lives.

I have two Kerry county championship medals and if things had gone our way a few other days, it could have been a return of four or five.

As it is, our club seemed to do well the years Kerry didn't.

After 1999, it was a big step up. In 2000, we came back and Fergal had us really fit. We got to the West Kerry final, the county senior championship final and the Millennium Cup final – which was a great FA Cup-style competition – and we ended up losing them all.

Kerry won the All-Ireland that year and it can't have helped us. You must celebrate an All-Ireland.

You always look at these things afterwards and say, 'How could we have done something different there?'

At the same time, the club was putting in brilliant structures and resources. We were getting stuff that no club player was ever getting. The club had attracted generous sponsorship, and us players were getting fed after training in what was a new hotel built down from the pitch, Carraig an Fhíona. We were even being sponsored a pair of Puma King football boots each which was amazing.

As well as that we had new thinking on the sideline. Fergal was in charge but he was still an important player too. He was free of injury, and An Ghaeltacht felt they needed a manager. Fergal was still coach, but Séamus Mac Gearailt, a man who had won All-Irelands with Kerry in 1969 and 1970 came in as manager.

He was Gaeltacht through and through and living in Tralee and he was the coach with Páidí in 1997 when Kerry won the All-Ireland. He had the credentials.

He brought a level of professionalism and structure but as well as that he'd encourage the players to talk and decide on things too. Figure it out yourselves, was his approach sometimes.

We reaped the benefits of all that work in 2001 when we came back and won the club championship, the county championship and the West Kerry championship.

Darragh was central to getting us over the line, but in the lead-up to the game, we weren't sure what type of shape he was going to be in. The International Rules was played in Australia around this time.

Ireland had sent a serious team down there: Séamus Moynihan, Graham Gerraghty, Pádraig Joyce, Anthony Tohill, Trevor Giles, Seán Marty Lockhart, all these great players – just the best of the best playing in Ireland. They won the series.

They were tough games that weren't for the faint-hearted and we were hoping he'd come home unscathed and be fit getting off the place after a very long return trip. Not since Scott and Charlene's wedding in *Neighbours* had we followed events in Australia so closely.

After a long trip back, he landed home to us on the Thursday before the county final on the Sunday. We were worried about jet lag and tiredness generally after the tour and the trip.

As well as that, he was coming up against William Kirby in midfield, a great player who was Darragh's partner in centre field with Kerry for many years. We knew we were very much up against it.

When Stacks get to the county finals, more often than not they win them.

But Darragh came home in time and he delivered. My God, what a performance. A display for the ages – he was man of the match by a country mile.

Páidí was doing the co-commentary with TG4 and I often watch it back and smile. Brian Tyres is doing the commentary and Páidí predicts what's going to happen throughout the game.

Dara Ó Cinnéide is taking a free kick and Páidí says, *as Gaeilge*, 'I think this is a small bit outside of Dara's range. I'm not sure he'll get this.' And Cinnéide misses.

Páidí then predicts that Cinnéide's going to get two tougher ones on the other side. And then Brian Tyres in the middle of the commentary, turns around to him, '*Níl scór deireanach agat, Pháidí* [You don't have the end score of the game by any chance, Páidí]?'

The make-up of the team too spoke to the close links of our parishes in west Kerry and the families that make up the peninsula. There was an Ó Sé, Breathnach and Ó Concubhar in every line of the field.

As Cyril Farrell said of his Galway team: we won everything but the Booker Prize that year.

The place went mad, and we did too. We'd finally won the county final. The celebrations were just amazing – the colour, the music. It was incredible. There were bonfires lit for us coming back west. We'd have a good relationship with Lispole and they had the way home lit for us.

We have a keen rivalry with Dingle and at the time they hadn't won a county championship in a long time. It'd be natural if it galled them to see us make the breakthrough first. But in fairness to them, there were bonfires through Dingle too. We came back home and going over the bridge with the cup was special.

As well as that first night's celebration, we had to visit all the parishes in the days and weeks afterwards. True to the club's motto, we took more than a sup on those days. There was a party in every parish.

At one stage after days of this, we were hopping into a

car at Ard an Bhóthair and my father came out to the road looking at us saying, 'Jesus Christ, are ye going again? There can't be anywhere left to go.'

We deserved to celebrate the historic win and it was a special time for the club but it caught up with us.

Getting to play in the Munster championship was a new experience but we weren't tuned in at all. You can see the same thing happen every year in the provincial championships.

We had the small matter of facing up to Nemo Rangers in Páirc Uí Chaoimh. They had the experience; they were going into that game rested and we most certainly were not going in fresh. Even though it was two weeks since the county final, we were still beering the week after the game.

So, the preparation going into that game against Nemo wasn't good at all but we nearly caught them late on – Tommy Beag Ó Muircheartaigh came off the bench and blasted a shot against the crossbar. If we'd had our heads screwed on, who knows what would have happened.

Lesson learned.

We vowed it would be different in 2003 when we won the title again.

A year earlier, we were beaten by Kilcummin in the county semi-final – it was pure complacency on our behalf.

Then the Kerins O'Rahillys beat us in the 2002 club final, but Darragh wasn't playing.

It was the week after the All-Ireland final against Armagh and we were completely flat. We threw it away that year but were determined to come back again in 2003.

It was the year of Páidí's painful departure from Kerry and we threw that fuel on the fire.

Laune Rangers had quality players like Mike Frank Russell and the Hassetts but we felt we had the better team overall.

I was marking Mike Frank in the drawn match and didn't do great. In the replay I got to grips with him and, the same way Darragh was the standout player in the 2001 final, this time Tomás put in an incredible performance.

Fergal was playing in the half back line, I was full back, Tomás was centre back and Darragh was midfield – so the four of us were starting in the county final and it was special to be on the field together, the four of us at the end. Darragh was captain and became the second An Ghaeltacht man to lift the Bishop Moynihan.

The night before the All-Ireland final, Mícheál Ó Sé gave us a speech that had us feeling we could run through the wall.

Tom Long, Mícheál, Liam Ó Rócháin, Francie Dorgan, Paddy Jack Ó Cinnéide – we had passionate West Kerry men on our backroom team.

Mícheál brought it back to *caid* and the ancient game between the parishes and where we came from, how we had been the bottom of the pecking order and how much this journey meant to our people.

It was highly emotional stuff, and it got us to a high emotional pitch.

If there were ever two people I've been involved with who could get you going for a game it's Mícheál and my uncle, Páidí. They were two fellas who'd inspire you before a game.

We reached Croke Park after taking the Munster campaign seriously. We ended up beating Kilkee of Clare in the Munster final. I was marking a fellow O'Shea, Michael, who's sadly died since of cancer. He was an excellent footballer for his club and Clare.

We were expected to lose in the semi-final against St Brigid's of Dublin, who had my college mate Barry Cahill. We managed to get past them in Thurles and myself and Barry were back in Maynooth together the following week. It's mad how the GAA works – I was in the St Brigid's club bar with Barry and some other Brigid's boys 24 hours later discussing the game.

And then you're in an All-Ireland club final, and the build-up and razzmatazz before that was just insane and something that we'd never experienced before.

There were people flying home from Australia, people flying home from America, lads coming out of the woodwork who'd been in London for decades. Our small club in the west of Kerry was in an All-Ireland senior final in Croke Park. It doesn't get much better and we knew these opportunities don't come around often.

It was about a bigger thing than winning a game of football too. This was about giving our people something to be proud of. We wanted to create something that they could look back on in 50 years' time.

We were an experienced outfit at this stage and we were confident going into that final.

It was some journey. I'll never forget seeing people play accordions in the stands at those Munster championship games or the number of people getting on buses at Moran's petrol station in Dingle, and the colours flying all over the peninsula. It gave us a great boost as well.

I always loved coming into Croke Park, through the streets of Dublin's northside and seeing the buzz around the place. There were 45,000 at Croke Park that day and a lot of them walked through without paying when the turnstiles malfunctioned and they opened the gates.

We were playing Caltra of Galway, who were a similar outfit to us – a real country club, backboned by a couple of families. It wasn't fair or accurate but it was billed in the media as the Ó Sés versus the Meehan brothers.

For us, though, one of our Ó Sés wasn't at 100 per cent. Darragh had injured himself in 2003 for the championship with Kerry. His fellow Kerry midfielder, Mike Quirke – a big man – fell on top of him and Darragh ended up with some bone bruising in his ankle. Darragh was never himself that year, never able to hit the heights that he did the years previously or did again in succeeding years.

I'm not making excuses, but I know that we would have been far better if he was at his best.

Caltra had their homework done too and came with a plan. They put Tomás Meehan on Darragh for the final and he did a man-marking role on him.

They also evidently targeted Tomás and his sorties up the field, knowing he was our main man that year.

The number of fellas who did third-man tackles on him coming up the field was unreal and ultimately, he lashed out. The ref gave Tomás a yellow card and if it wasn't exactly the end of him, it curtailed his influence afterwards.

We lost by a point in the end – the key moment was an off-balance Ó Cinnéide swinging a goal chance over the bar, under pressure.

It was devastating at the final whistle and it was devastating for our people. We obviously wanted to do it for ourselves but we wanted to do it for our families and the people like Liam Ó Rócháin, Mícheál Ó Sé and Tom Ó Cruadhlaoich who'd got us there.

'*An mbeimíd thar nais aríst* [Will we be back again]?' one of the lads asked Ó Cinnéide as we watched the trophy presentation from the pitch.

An optimist – or maybe just a kind soul – he said, 'We will.' I think we all knew that it was unlikely for a club like ours to get this chance again. It's the biggest regret of my career not winning that one.

If we'd lost by 20 points it'd be easier to take and it might not intrude on my thoughts late at night, as it often does now. If you ask me now, would I take the All-Ireland club final in 2004 or would I take an All-Ireland with Kerry, I'd happily toss a Celtic Cross onto the table and take that title with the club.

CHAPTER 12

THE BIG SHOW

I'm not sure if the fact that Páidí was in charge helped or hindered me – I suspect the latter – but I managed to get Kerry trials in 2000.

From then on, I was in and about the panel for the next 16 years.

When Darragh made his breakthrough in the 1993–94 season, he came into a dressing room that was not a happy place after years of underachievement, in the eyes of the Kerry public. They turned that around and by the time I pushed open the door, it was a great time to be involved because Kerry were flying.

Still, there were only 24 on the panel and it was hard enough to establish yourself. As well as that, I was very much a late developer. In 2001, I was training a lot with the team and still not making that breakthrough. Kerry beat Cork in a Munster final and played Dublin in a novel quarter-final in Thurles.

After an epic draw, famous for Maurice Fitzgerald's memorable kick from the sideline at the death, we had to go again. I wasn't involved with the panel on the day and went to the game with my dad.

The first game was tasty enough and the Dubs' manager Tommy Carr was watching the replay from the stands subsequently. Tomás kicked things off again by making a reckless trip on Colin Moran as the Dublin forward was running through on goal.

Páidí went ballistic on the sideline as Tomás was sent off by Pat McEnaney and he had to be held back by the linesmen. My dad was almost inconsolable next to me, rubbing his head and looking out at this vista. 'Oh, my God. What is after happening here?'

We watched in silence as Tomás sat into the bench and this win-or-bust championship game resumed without him. But after a minute or two of evaluating the situation, I said, 'Jesus, Tomás will be gone the next day, dad. There'll be a defender needed. This could be my chance to break through!'

My father looked at me working this out in real time with a look as if to say, 'Will you shut the fuck up?' As it happened, Kerry got past that Dublin team and I *was* in the 24 for the Meath game, the infamous day when the Royals annihilated Kerry.

The Hogan Stand was being built and I was sitting in the dugout in the Cusack Stand. To my shame, the hiding got so bad from the Royals that towards the end I started to hope I wouldn't be called to go on.

But that was my first ever day with the seniors in Croke Park. I suppose I can thank my brother. I aimed to get back there for better days.

When I was in and around the Kerry panel in 2001, Páidí made sure I was in the right position to learn quickly.

We had a challenge match in Meath and were to travel in cars, a practice Páidí reintroduced. Like Jose Mourinho, he parked the bus. The convoy of cars was a throwback to the Micko days and it worked well.

The West Kerry car, at that time, was filling up and the pecking order was well settled.

Páidí was in the driving seat in more ways than one, Darragh stretched out in the front seat, Tomás, Aodán and Ó Cinnéide were in the back. Four in the back would have been a bit of a squeeze, so when we got as far as Castleisland, Páidí said to me, hop in there with Séamus Moynihan, who was leaning on his car.

As I got out of our car, Páidí caught me by the elbow and gave me some instructions. 'When you get in there with Moynihan, just be a sponge,' he said. 'Learn as much as you can from him.'

Johnny McGlynn was driving and Noel Kennelly and Séamus Scanlon were folded into the back with me. We headed off and if I ever did anything in my life, I would have made sure that I followed Páidí's directions that day. I just watched everything Séamus did on that journey and thereafter for years; the way he carried himself, the way he walked, the way he'd catch a ball, the way he'd kick it. Everything.

I don't think there's any player, except for Pat Spillane, who only had one foot like that. Obviously, there are players that only have one foot, but for them to be *as good* as they were with just one foot – Spillane and Moynihan were probably the best ever. That's not faint praise. He was an amazing player who I just loved playing with.

That first journey together, however, wasn't without its bumps in the road. We got as far as north Tipperary and we started chugging and the dash lit up with warning lights. The car broke down and we pulled in, putting in a call to Páidí who, of course, had all the contacts throughout the country.

He gave us the name of a garage that he was familiar with not far away from where we'd stalled and this character kindly came out to help. We explained we had a game to get to and he gave us an old estate car to get us up to Navan.

We were like kids giggling in the back of this thing, which jolted violently backwards and forwards every time Johnny pressed on the accelerator. We were rocking back and forth up the road, in stitches. We didn't know if we were going to get to the game at all but we eventually pulled into the ground in a cloud of smoke, roaring laughing.

*

I had been around the panel the year before but it was my first time properly getting to bond with these fellas.

I played around a half hour and, though it was just a challenge match, it was my first game with the Kerry seniors and I'll always remember it. At one stage, Johnny was bearing down on goal and Darren Fay, a fearsome competitor for Meath over the years, was coming out to put in the tackle and snuff out the danger.

But Johnny put on the afterburners and he just about got to the ball first and lashed it to the back of the net. It was an unbelievable goal – and, as importantly, he avoided getting clattered by Fay.

Coming down again in the estate, we congratulated Johnny on a great goal and he was rightly delighted with his performance. When we got to Castleisland again, I was transferred back to the West Kerry motor.

We were heading out the road west and I remarked, 'Johnny got a great goal, didn't he?' Páidí looked at me in the rearview mirror and said, 'He had two choices. Keep going at the pace he was going and end up in the Mater Private or put the boot down.' I learned a lot that day.

CHAPTER 13

AT THE CROSSROADS

On a wet Sunday morning, we watched Ireland lose to Spain on penalties in the 2002 World Cup in Japan and then went out to play Cork.

We drew eight points apiece, and I marked a real knacky, townie forward, Fionán Murray. I didn't do too much on the day and Fionán didn't do much either. We'd have another chance to make an impression at least. A few days later my father passed away.

It was sudden. I took a phone call from Páidí with the message that something had happened to Dad and when I got back to the house at Ard an Bhóthair there was an ambulance parked up outside.

Páidí and our neighbour Mícheál Ó Sé came out of the door with their arms around each other. I knew straight away. I sat down on a bench in the corner of my mother's garden to compose myself before going in to face it.

We buried him on the Thursday and that evening the three of us – myself, Darragh and Tomás – decided we were going to play Cork in the replay on the Saturday.

There were three players on the Kerry team bereaved, plus the manager. But the Munster Council weren't prepared to put the match back a week. Not that we asked for or expected any dispensations.

My mother left the decision to us – 'You lads decide if you'll play.' But she did say that dad would have wanted us to line out and I think he would have too.

Once the decision was made at the funeral, we realised if we were going to play in Cork at the weekend, we'd better go to training.

There were a lot of Kerry supporters who said that they wouldn't travel because they were going to take a stance against the game going ahead. I think the Kerry supporters should have travelled to support us – that's when we needed them. But I got their point.

An impressive delegation of Cork GAA people arrived in Ventry for the funeral, which was appreciated. You wouldn't expect anything less.

The likes of Dr Con Murphy, Billy Morgan, Frank Murphy and Larry Tompkins, who was the manager of Cork at the time, all made the long journey. So too did a lot of the Cork players, which was noted. There were GAA people from all over coming through the house.

I came into the kitchen at one stage and Páidí and his old manager Mick O'Dwyer were giggling like schoolboys.

I was away at college at the time and Páidí had arranged with Micko that I'd train with his Kildare team during the week.

I had thought this would be straightforward enough because I was in Maynooth and they trained in Newbridge – how hard could that be? I figured out where exactly I needed to get to and how I'd negotiate it on public transport. I left at around 5 p.m. after a college lecture and thought I'd be there in fine time but I turned up to this inter-county session late.

I had to get around two or three buses to get there and was fairly stressed out before I pulled on the boots. I eventually got on the pitch, fell in and it became apparent this was old-school training from Micko's Golden Years playbook. It was all laps and laps of the pitch and a bit of football at the end, which was all good, and you could see he was getting these lads fit.

Micko came up to me afterwards and said in his familiar voice, 'Well Marc, did you enjoy that?'

I said, 'I loved it, Mick, thanks very much for having me,' and had a bit of grub afterwards with him.

But then I started to think how the hell am I going to get back to Maynooth again here. It was all hours of the morning before I got back to my digs. I never went back.

Newbridge or nowhere? Nowhere, please. Páidí had gone out on a limb to ask his old manager for a favour and Kildare were accommodating me but I said to myself, *Look, this isn't working out here. I'm just going to have to train hard while I'm on my own.* I was as fit as anyone and I trained diligently on my own.

I neglected to tell Páidí that I couldn't hack catching multiple Bus Éireann coaches in the dark so I could run laps twice a week. Then I walked in on this old pair of friends as they were having a cup of tea at the kitchen table in our homeplace.

'Fair play to you Mick,' Páidí said in a stage whisper loud enough so I could hear him as I boiled the kettle again, 'you had this fellow with you for the couple of months.'

But Micko said, 'Jesus, we thought we'd see more of him. He was only there once or twice. He's a rogue like the rest of you.' The two were just laughing; they'd clearly been tick-tacking before then and Páidí knew well that I wasn't turning up. But he trusted I was training away. I would have heard all about it otherwise.

The funeral was the Thursday morning and we went over to training that evening.

It was a very tough week, of course, and it was hard to feel motivated as we left the family home to get into the car and leave. When we got there the lads had already started and had their warm-up done as we were a bit late. It's a lonely place to be too, being outside the group.

But I'll never forget the feeling when we went onto the field because the three of us needed to warm-up together. Without saying a whole lot, we formed a tight circle and started kicking the ball between us on this summer's evening in Fitzgerald's Stadium.

Kick, catch, kick, catch. It was like being back in my parents' garden as young lads, just getting satisfaction from the act of kicking a ball to your brothers. People talk about mindfulness nowadays – I think people were practising it way before we had a name; whether that's playing an accordion or striking a ball against a gable end.

Then we rejoined the group.

Nothing was going to change in our lives over the course of an hour and we'd be back to reality soon enough. But all the troubles of the week, all the thoughts and sadness just went away for that short period of time.

It was a quick session because the game was on Saturday but my mind was clear until the whistle went again.

I was poor in the replay. I'm not sure if the toll of the week told on my body but my legs felt like jelly. We didn't have a drink all week but you wouldn't be sleeping and everyone knows how emotionally intense those periods are. We were drained.

A ball or two came down the wing, and I felt like I was running through treacle. I was being twisted and turned and I just couldn't keep at it.

Before the throw in, the announcer came on and said, 'We're going to have a minute's silence now for Michael Ó Sé, who passed away this week.'

Colin Corkery, who was full forward ran over to my corner and shook my hand and just tapped me on the head. I thought it was just an amazing sporting gesture, from an incredible man. A class act.

But the game goes on and Corkery was ruthless and a big part of the reason that Cork won easily. They celebrated wildly, which was right.

After an emotional week, a huge shock, we'd face into the back door and see where it took us.

Atter we played that replay there was a lot of talk around the place suggesting that Fionán Murray had said something to me during 'Amhrán na bhFiann'.

I heard the story back weeks and weeks later. This version was that Fionán had nudged me during the anthem and said something along the lines of 'My father's above in the stand there, where's your father?' That was absolute bullshit but people still say it to me to this day.

None of the Cork lads said *anything* like that. There was huge respect shown, which we really appreciated. It's just what you'd expect from GAA people and Irish people.

But it was a lesson in how these crazy rumours go around – and what people are willing to believe.

CHAPTER 14

THE WRONG TROUSERS

If I was able to reel back the tape and change how any match played out for me, it'd be an All-Ireland final – my first.

After my father died, we went on a run that saw us produce some of the best football I saw any Kerry side play. Of course it was a tough time. You're not sleeping properly; you're probably still in shock a little and grieving as a young man. But I think football got us through that time.

The route back to the final took us around the country; we had Wicklow, then Fermanagh – where I picked up my first man-of-the-match award – then Kildare.

We took on the 2001 All-Ireland champions, Galway, and absolutely blitzed them in the quarter-final. We played great football and won comfortably in the end by eight points, with Aodán Mac Gearailt scoring a goal and point and Darragh and Tomás also getting on the scoresheet.

Next up it was Cork again in the All-Ireland semi-final. Our old rivals had beaten us already, of course, but we were fired up for this one. We weren't going to be beaten by our neighbours in Croke Park.

Gooch and Mike Frank put on a master display in that game, scoring 2–11 between them – and we got through: 3–19 to 2–7.

Páidí admitted afterwards that we wanted to make it payback time for the Rebels. His old boss Mick O'Dwyer evoked Michael O'Hehir's famous line about his Kerry team of the 1970s: 'And now they're really rolling.' But I didn't play great. I was taken off in the 53rd minute for Tom O'Sullivan. My graph was trending downwards over the course of the run.

As we came back down the road, I wondered if I'd be in the team for the final against Armagh.

I'd grown up hearing about my uncle play – and win – All-Ireland finals and later watching my brothers line out in our game's biggest day.

Now I'd join them.

It brought a new pressure and hype, of course. In the run up to the big day I made the rookie mistake of focusing on the post All-Ireland final function that was on the night of the game – the same type of one that I broke into in 1997 – and I was looking for tickets.

'Don't be worrying about those old bits of cardboard,' Páidí said angrily when he picked up on what was happening. 'Jesus Christ, what are you doing? Forget about that. Focus on the match,' he said.

He gave me a proper bollocking, which I took on board. Darragh and Tomás were very supportive and I leaned on them. I knew that the selector John O'Keeffe was fond of me and rated me as a player and I suspected he would fight my corner when it came to a team selection conversation.

With my uncle as manager, I felt you had to be nearly twice as good as anyone else to get the benefit of the doubt, but John's opinion would have validated a decision for Páidí. He respected his opinion completely.

I got the nod in the end and my brief was simple going into the big day: keep my man scoreless and stop them playing.

Despite the counsel to focus on preparation and the match, I realised I made a schoolboy error when I opened my kitbag in the Croke Park dressing room.

I'd generally be very particular and would have my stuff carefully packed. Being meticulous at putting my gear together was part of a process of preparation for me, I know now.

But on this occasion, when I pulled out the jocks, I realised they were comically big and different ones to what I'd usually wear. They were coming down over the togs inside and I was preoccupied with it and uncomfortable. A small thing but not how you want to start your first All-Ireland.

The next mistake I made was thinking the game was won at half time.

We came in four points up at the break and I thought there was no way we could let it slip. I was this complacent young fella, thinking we'd this game won.

I was in completely the wrong mindset and that's something I learned from and it helped me later – but the lesson came at an expensive price.

In the run up to the final I was marking the Gooch in training. He was already one of the top forwards in the game but he was probably ten and a half stone.

I wasn't much heavier at that stage.

On All-Ireland Sunday, I trotted out and shook hands with my direct opponent, Diarmaid Marsden. Woah … he made an impression straight away. He was a big man and a different proposition to Colm.

Looking back, I think I would have benefitted from tuning up against Dara Ó Cinnéide or Johnny Crowley or one of those bigger lads in our camp. Later in my career – fast forward almost a decade to the 2011 final against

Dublin, for example – I was 13 or 13 and a half stone nearly.

If you're two and a half stone heavier, you can protect the ball better, you can hold people up in the tackle, you have loads of advantages and I just didn't have that bulk in 2002.

I had the skillset and I was able to play but I was fighting up a few weight classes against a good footballer. A good big man always beats a good little man, as the boxing adage goes.

As well as that, fatigue set in.

We'd been on a white-knuckle rollercoaster ride all summer. Football kept us going after my father's sudden death and we were kept busy with a packed itinerary of games, but it was catching up with me.

Marsden got two points off me in the first half but we still had that four-point advantage at half time.

In the full back line in general, we were taking on water. Mike McCarthy was on Stevie McDonald, Séamus Moynihan was marking Ronan Clarke and I was trying to curb Diarmaid Marsden's influence.

Between that trio of Armagh forwards, they kicked nine points – three off each of us. Of the three of us, Páidí called me to the sideline in the second half – subbed off in my first All-Ireland.

It's a tough place to be, sitting on the bench as the game slips away. You're in the stand for the last 15, 20 minutes, helpless.

And when that goal goes in for Armagh through Oisín

McConville, they have all the momentum and it's a case of trying to keep the tide out again.

I was just clenching my legs in the stand and feeling exhausted and completely useless.

There are huge what-ifs there. *What if I'd done this? What if I'd done that?* I felt at the time that I'd let the side down, and I think I did. That was the one game that went away from me – it just happened to be my first final.

I don't think I've ever watched the Armagh 2002 one back again properly. I just can't face it.

But I've probably seen enough of it over the years. There was plenty of video analysis done afterwards and Páidí and later Jack would have picked parts in the game you'd look at.

We played Armagh in the league the following year in Tralee and I got a goal in the last minute to win it. It was a league game but I took satisfaction from that moment and used it to draw a line and move on.

Anytime I came up against them afterwards, I was going to make sure I played well.

But that Armagh final, I've literally had nightmares about it, thinking about the way I was defending. Maybe, as they say, you have to lose one to win one. I ultimately had to lose four to win five, so maybe that checks out.

I was featured on *Laochra Gael* in 2025 and had to revisit a lot of match footage as part of the process. Watching those moments from the 2002 final made me emotional.

I see a slip of a lad trying to get through his first All-Ireland, which had footballing disadvantages. But I also see a young man dealing with the trauma of losing his father suddenly.

What also gets me is that Darragh was captain. He was such a brilliant player and leader for us but he never got to lift the Sam Maguire as Kerry skipper. It's one of the biggest regrets of my career. I'm sorry we couldn't do it for him.

After a challenging year, I was looking forward to blowing off some steam with a trip to South Africa.

It had been a tough season but I'd established myself in the team and was optimistic I'd kick on with Páidí and the rest of the lads.

It was my first trip away with the panel and I was rooming with Gooch.

He was deadly – we'd have these two big suitcases at the end of the bed and we'd go out on a given night and he would just come over to my suitcase and put on my jeans and shirt and he's gone. As elusive off the field nicking my bootcuts as he was that season on the pitch.

I'd pick up the pants the next day off the floor and the end of them destroyed from going under his shoes as he traipsed around the place.

We were in the same hotel as the Kilkenny hurlers and the Dublin football team at the same time. A few days in, the resort staff made it known that there'd been some damage to the pool.

As Tony Soprano asked his son in the principal's office, 'How can you vandalise a swimming pool?'

The hotel manager was furious and fingered a red-haired suspect as the one who'd thrown some furniture into the water.

Now, between us, we had plenty of red heads. Think the opening scene in *The Usual Suspects* but with more freckles.

We had Gooch, Noel Kennelly, Liam Hassett and Séamus Scanlon. And it could plausibly have been any of those four because they were a quartet of absolute lunatics. Kilkenny had a few red-haired candidates too – and the Dubs.

There was a sit-down organised. Páidí brought Kilkenny boss Brian Cody and Dublin manager Tommy Lyons together.

'Look,' he said, 'there was something broken. It doesn't matter who it was. We're all representing the GAA and the country. We need to just go 33 per cent each here and have done with it.'

Tommy Lyons says, 'Yeah, no bother, Páidí.'

But Cody wasn't keen, 'No, I'm not happy to do that at all.' And, then, with a Colombo-like reveal, didn't Páidí turn around and whisper, 'Look Brian, I didn't want to say it, but it was actually Henry Shefflin that did it.'

It wasn't at all true. But the thing was settled between the three men.

A little while later, I was lying on the bed while Colm was pottering around the room when the door nearly came off the hinges and Páidí came in on top of us.

'Gooch,' Páidí barked, 'I don't want to see you around the fucking place for the next few days.'

Like Shefflin, Colm wasn't at all involved in this minor incident – but Páidí thought it best Gooch keep a low profile until things blew over.

'Or if you do go out, put a cap on,' Páidí said, over his shoulder as he left. 'Good man.'

Of course, when we visited Robben Island, our own prisoner was referenced. We visited various national parks, a bar or two and the Irish embassy. It was a great trip.

Then Marty Morrissey showed up and things went pear-shaped.

Páidí had called the Kerry supporters 'fucking animals' in an interview in the *Sunday Independent*.

The well-known journalist Kevin Kimmage rang the bar in the days after Christmas of 2002 and asked Páidí if he could arrange a feature interview with Darragh. 'Sure, interview me,' Páidí said.

The writer came to Ventry and during the conversation, Páidí said, 'We didn't win the All-Ireland last year so it didn't matter whether we lost by one point or 50. That's not acceptable to Kerry supporters. People will say that we're great losers and all to that, we are gracious in defeat but deep down, Kerry people don't like to lose.

'Being Kerry manager is probably the hardest job in the

world because Kerry people, I'd say, are the roughest type of fucking animals you could ever deal with.

'And you can print that.'

The *Sunday Independent* did print it. But we were completely oblivious as to what was unfolding. First, this was a time before smartphones, news apps and WhatsApp. Secondly, we were having the time of our lives and enjoying everything Cape Town had to offer. Though Dara Ó Cinnéide had mentioned to me that there might be some bother.

He'd printed out the interview in an internet cafe and told me broadly what Páidí had said. I remembered back to the day Páidí had brought Kevin Kimmage over the road to meet us brothers and our mother in our place a week or so earlier.

Looking at the printout with Dara, I said, 'Okay, there might be a bit of trouble here alright, but it'll go away – Páidí's survived a few scrapes worse than this before now.'

Little did we know that this was the beginning of the end for Páidí.

He spoke to Marty – who happened to be in South Africa anyway – and the county board put out a statement. I don't think Páidí, or the rest of us, understood the depth of feeling and the controversy that was brewing at home.

It's like Castleisland man Con Houlihan said: 'I missed Italia '90. I was in Italy.'

Back home the radio shows, local media and national sports pages were brimming with debate over this 'animals' remark. Páidí ate humble pie and earned a stay of execution. The episode cost him a lot of political capital however and there was no room for error now in the coming season.

2003 was a case of second-season syndrome for me, after the rollercoaster the year before.

I was playing well in the Munster championship campaign but contracted glandular fever and I got very sick around Easter time and I had to go to the hospital. I was in hospital for the bones of a week and I was told my spleen was swollen. 'Is your spleen swollen or are you just pleased to see me?' one of the lads said.

I wasn't allowed to play football for a month or so until the spleen came back to size so I missed out on a bit there and obviously gave up my place.

I got back onto a pitch eventually and earned my place with Kerry but I wasn't right. The thing had wiped me of any strength and energy.

We played Roscommon in the quarter-final and I was wing back and I was whipped after 20-odd minutes in the first half. And deservedly so.

Páidí dropped me for what would be his final Kerry game in charge. We'd face Tyrone, who'd become very familiar in the succeeding years, but I started the afternoon watching from the Hogan Stand. After 27 or 28 minutes, John Sheehan was struggling and I was sent on.

I soon realised what we were facing. I was marking a Tyrone player and the first ball that came out, Darragh was jumping for it. As we were waiting for the ball to break, the Tyrone player turned to me and grabbed me by the belly like you'd catch a dog by the scruff. He pinched as hard as he could, or so it felt.

I quickly made the decision to match fire with fire and caught his belly and did the same.

Before half time I managed to go up the field and get a point which was always something that gave me great confidence and I felt great. The same Tyrone player got a point off me as well in the second half and Tyrone turned the screw. In the end, we got mauled.

A Kerry supporter – a man in his 50s – hopped the fence a few minutes from the end of play and hit Páidí. I couldn't believe it.

Speaking to reporters afterwards, Páidí tried to laugh it off, saying he probably deserved a 'haymaker' after all his years in Croke Park.

We flew home from Dublin airport, and Páidí was sitting next to me on the plane. He must have been suffering after a bad defeat like that and perhaps he knew his time was up. But he leant over to me and said, 'You answered your critics today. Well done.'

I heard him say once that there are only three things of which a Kerryman is afraid: 'Bad porter, a parish priest's housekeeper and a rusty razor.' We weren't going to back down against Armagh, Tyrone and this new breed of Ulster sides.

It meant everything to me to get his validation and it gave me a big boost. As we descended into Farranfore after another season, I was still without a Celtic Cross. I was full of self-doubt and nagging questions.

But him saying that about my performance against Tyrone boosted my confidence. Though we'd lost, I'd played well and stood up against Tyrone. In the years afterwards, for some reason, I always played well and I never took a backward step against them.

I finished the year knowing I was more trusted as a Kerry player. I had been struggling because of illness but I was able to get back and help the team and do well in the Tyrone match. I was able to do well in a county final replay. And I think that that stood to me for 2004.

It's hard to explain now what the atmosphere in the county was like in the time after that defeat to Tyrone.

Radio Kerry was inundated with calls and texts, asking if Páidí should stay or go. He had the backing of 52 per cent of the respondents.

Former teammates were having their say in the media, the airwaves were full of commentary, and of course, he was still trying to run a pub. The stress on him must have been intense.

Having to front up there in the bar wasn't easy. When things went badly for Kerry – and that means not winning an All-Ireland – Páidí took it worse than anyone, but he had to pull the shutters up each day.

It was the end of the road for him as Kerry manager. His days were probably numbered since the 'Kerry animals' controversy, which was blown out of proportion. Then when we ran into another chainsaw of an Ulster team, it was a handy decision for the people in power.

Not that they handled it well – or in a way that someone who'd given so much to Kerry football deserved. Somebody rang Páidí to tell him that he was going to be sacked here. It was a third party rather than the county board chairman informing him, in a dignified way, of his fate.

I know I'm biased but I think it's a real shame that he was ultimately let go when he was – there was another All-Ireland in that team under Páidí.

He had won two All-Irelands for Kerry as manager – ending what we'd consider here a famine – 11 summers. We were unlucky against Armagh in 2002. But if you were to look at a poor run of results over the course of three years it was going to come to a head and I don't think the comments about the supporters helped him in that situation.

Maybe had he not expressed himself in that way, he might have got away with it.

If he'd stayed, he would have changed things up. We did have to evolve our style, certainly, to come up against the new breed in Armagh and Tyrone; I think Páidí would have enjoyed that challenge and he might have freshened up his backroom team to get newer perspectives on the game.

The way Páidí was dealt with wasn't right and we found that hard to swallow. And it took Páidí a while to get over how it ended. I wouldn't blame him that he was bitter for a while afterwards over that – though I know that didn't last.

But he went up then straight away to Westmeath, taking over as manager. And to do what he did then up there, winning a Leinster title, it was him giving two fingers to the Kerry county board.

He illustrated how good he was as a manager, showing the county board representatives or whoever it was who'd sacked him.

I never told him afterwards, but when they lost to Derry in the All-Ireland quarter-final in 2004, I was glad they did. We played Derry in the semi-final. I wouldn't have enjoyed coming up against Páidí instead. Beating our uncle would not have been enjoyable. But it would have been worse to lose to him.

CHAPTER 15

A TIDE IN THE AFFAIRS OF MEN

We were still Kerry footballers, however. Jack O'Connor was appointed, which wasn't surprising, and it was clear he viewed the three of us – the Ó Sés – as a cabal that needed to be managed, given he'd just replaced our uncle.

We held nothing against Jack, rather the way Páidí's departure was handled was what rankled. Darragh, then one of the top players in the country, wasn't happy with the way it played out, but he had more influence. I was this new kid on the block, whereas his voice would have been heard and people would have known that he wasn't too impressed.

Quite apart from Jack, it was difficult to look on as the people who got rid of Páidí were still there. But of course, we were never a team, or a set of brothers, who were into player power. It was raw but we moved forward tentatively with Jack. He'd need us and we'd need him if we were to win an All-Ireland.

I had great roommates over the years like the Gooch in South Africa or later Eoin Brosnan, who I roomed with for 13 happy seasons. But when I started out, I was still that sponge that Páidí advised me to be with Séamus Moynihan.

It was a bit of a policy to have an older and a younger player in the one room. Jack took us away for a bonding weekend in Cork three weeks before the All-Ireland quarter-final against Dublin in 2004.

We stayed in the five-star Hayfield Manor no less and after training in the Mardyke we came back to the dining room where selector Ger O'Keefe had this great idea: we'd have a couple of glasses of wine with our meal.

What could possibly go wrong?

We were delighted. The food was beautiful and we all agreed the wine was very nice. Before we knew it, after this aperitif, the likes of myself, Tomás, Aidan O'Mahony and Mike McCarthy were climbing out windows and slipping out back doors. We were down in Preachers on Washington Street having a beer within a quarter of an hour.

The following day – when we were to train again – this group of budding sommeliers paid the price. I stuck my head in the door and Tomás was upside down inside in his room. Mike McCarthy wasn't much better. Neither made it down for the session.

The smell of drink from me inside in the hotel room, which I shared with Séamus, was cruel. But I got up out of the bed, trained and I think, for that effort alone, I went way up in Séamo's estimation.

Of course, we had to apologise. A week or so later, Jack walked into the meeting room where we were all gathered, nodded at us and said, 'Look, lads, not good enough.'

As we all had to take our turn to stand up and say sorry to the group, Séamus was sitting in front of me, arms folded, leaning back, taking this in. He had the two legs off the chair, like you'd see a student in school.

When it got to my turn in the circle of shame, I said, 'Lads, look, I apologise. I had a few glasses of the wine and I had a real taste for it.'

At that Moynihan just erupted laughing, threw his head back and fell off the chair into the group in a fit of giggles.

It broke the ice, everyone relaxed and we moved on – thankfully.

The group agreed that if we were going to give this a crack, we must toe the line and just do what we were doing on the training pitch. We went on to win the All-Ireland. Was it because we snuck out for a drink in Cork earlier in the year? That's not for me to say.

*

Generally, we lived like monks. That Dublin game was three weeks out anyway and I ended up playing well. Those moments are important in bonding a group too. We were getting a bit of a laugh out of the stuff that was going on.

Donaghy was new to the squad that time and was becoming a hugely important personality, as well as player, in the group. On that trip to the Hayfield Manor, Donaghy was under the impression that everything was free.

As we went out the door on the Sunday morning, his bag was completely packed. Ger O'Keeffe, the selector, who's a Stacks man as well as Donaghy, said, 'Woah, hold on there, Kieran … your bag.'

He opened up Donaghy's kitbag and it'd remind you of Axel Foley taking the robes from the Beverly Hills hotel. There were slippers, fluffy towels, shower gels, the whole lot of it stuffed in.

'Kieran, where are you going with that stuff?' Ger asked.

'Well, Ger,' Donaghy says innocently, as he pointed at two bathrobes, 'that's for my mother, and that's my grand-mother.'

And sure, we got weeks out of that one – little things like that are great entertainment and help bond a group together.

Páidí's mantra that you weren't a Kerry footballer until you had an All-Ireland was like a jingle I couldn't get out of my head.

Some nights I worried if it would ever come. We were late coming back to the county set up because of An Ghaeltacht's run to the All-Ireland final and I found myself on the outside. Jack was going to make me earn my place back.

I started the summer on the bench against Cork but an injury to Séamus Moynihan opened a door. I had my chance and vowed to give Jack no option but to keep me in the team.

One night before a championship game, chatting to my roommate Eoin Brosnan, I wondered aloud whether this All-Ireland medal would ever come my way.

When we beat Derry in the semi-final I vowed not to get distracted by tickets, to pack shorts that fit me and do my job on the pitch all the way until the final whistle.

When we blitzed Mayo in the first half of the final, I refused to let myself believe.

Two years previously I had stupidly thought Armagh were beaten at the break in the 2002 final. This time, with an even greater margin, I thought, *Time to just drive this home.*

There was a difference in maturity that wasn't there in 2002. When the whistle went, the overriding feeling was relief. There was pressure – I was putting it on myself – but soaking it up from family members unconsciously too.

But I had my medal and now I was a proper Kerry footballer.

*

Anyone who walked into my grandmother Beatrice's house would have known that the sitting room was a shrine to Páidí. And this photograph took centre stage. Beatrice would tell us it was like the Mona Lisa, in that anywhere you walked in the room, Páidí's eyes would follow you.

Pádraig Óg has done some great things with the pub. This is his latest venture with Páidí's collection of medals and the famous 1982 jersey from when Kerry were going for five-in-a-row. A fantastic feature in the pub that people get selfies with every day.

The four of us on Ventry Beach. We spent a lot of time during the summers down there going for jogs in our free time.

Páidí on the pitch before his biggest game of all, the 1985 All-Ireland final against Dublin, where he was captain. He really wanted to make sure that he performed well on the day and he certainly held up his end of the bargain. (© Ray McManus / SPORTSFILE)

Very much in the mould of our uncle Páidí, Tomás was a force to be reckoned with. He turned into an inspirational player for An Ghaeltacht and Kerry, and will be regarded as one of the greatest half backs of all time. (© Ray McManus / SPORTSFILE)

A warm embrace between Páidí and Darragh after the 1997 All-Ireland final. Páidí was the manager who broke the 11-year famine and brought Sam back to the Kingdom, with Darragh winning his first All-Ireland in the process. A great day for the house. (© David Maher / SPORTSFILE)

I lár na páirce. Darragh doing what he did best, getting high up into the sky and catching that ball. (© Ray McManus / SPORTSFILE)

All-Ireland club final in 2004 marking the great Michael Meehan. Always tough battles with Meehan. Caltra came out on top that day, which was a devastating loss for the Gaeltacht. We knew it would be difficult to get back there. (© Ray McManus / SPORTSFILE)

A National League game against Armagh in Tralee. Physically, I still had a lot of filling out to do in those early years. (© Brendan Moran / SPORTSFILE)

A media day before the All-Ireland final in 2009, with Tomás and Darragh. We used to call these events the Night of the Yerras. (© Brendan Moran / SPORTSFILE)

Winning the Texaco Player of the Year in 2007, alongside Cork's Angela Walsh and Waterford's Dan Shanahan. A wonderful night where Irish greats such as Pádraig Harrington and Brian O'Driscoll were also honoured. (© Brendan Moran / SPORTSFILE)

Hugely proud to win an All Star with Darragh and Tomás in 2007. Three brothers on the one All Star team was certainly one of the highlights of my career and this photo hangs proudly in the An Ghaeltacht clubhouse. (© Brendan Moran / SPORTSFILE)

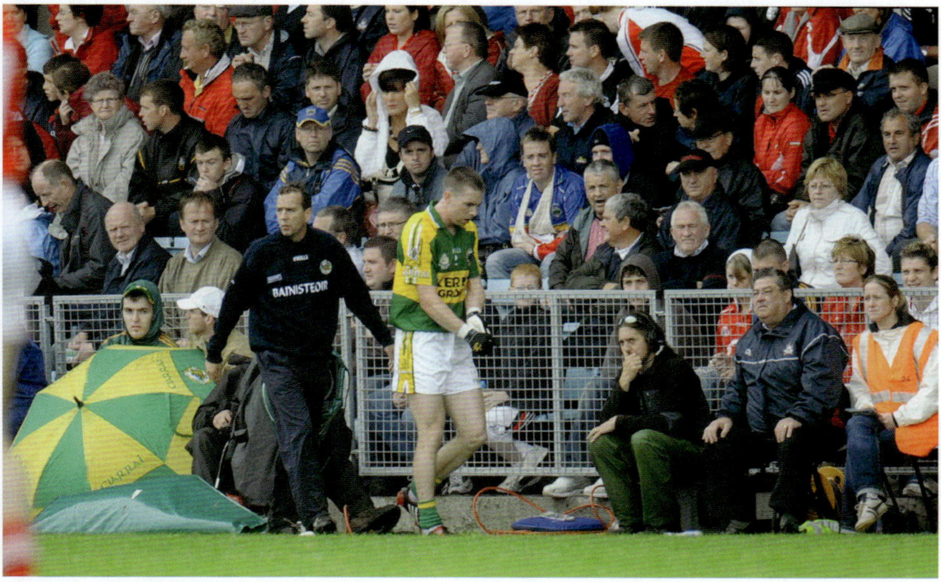

Sent off against Cork in the '08 Munster final. A red card that was overturned afterwards following a meeting with the CCCC. (© Stephen McCarthy / SPORTSFILE)

Fighting for the ball against Colm O'Neill. There were many tough battles with Cork forwards down through the years. (© Brendan Moran / SPORTSFILE)

Captaining Kerry in the '09 Munster final in Páirc Uí Chaoimh. A huge honour. (© Brendan Moran / SPORTSFILE)

By 2006, we were in bad shape. We had Waterford first out in Munster and they were winning that game at one stage. Though we got the job done in the end, there was war after the game in the old dressing rooms in Fitzgerald Stadium.

Seán Walsh was the chairman and himself and Jack O'Connor were arguing and he stormed out. But he went out the front door and came back in through the physio's room and we all lost the plot laughing and roaring at each other.

It didn't feel like a very aligned, high-performance environment at that stage of the summer. But I think everyone was just frustrated after that game because we were poor.

We were coming off a year that still stung, having lost the final in 2005 to Tyrone.

Séamus Moynihan, by his standards, was poor at the end of the year because his back was in a bad way. He wasn't the Séamo that we knew; he had the handbrake three-quarters of the way up, through no fault of his own. The body just wasn't allowing him to operate.

He went on a programme with the physio Ger Keane and he worked so hard during the winter on his core, to make sure that he came back in 2006 in far better shape. And he did.

But at the start of the year in 2006, he broke down again and we thought, *Is this the end of Séamo?* But he made it back for the championship.

Personally, I felt I was well established. I had put on

weight in the previous couple of years and I had my Celtic Cross.

I loved getting up the field and I felt I had the ball playing to have an effect in other positions but at the same time I loved defending. John O'Keefe was always in my ear telling me to do the simple things right and take pride in the art of defending. He was preaching to the converted.

I always watched old clips of Kerry players, even Kerry's Golden Years, and studied how they performed. Páidí used to tell me that a forward would be at his most vulnerable when he is about to take that solo or hop or try to get a shot away. That's when you pounce, if you can.

I'll never forget the clip of John O'Keefe marking the great dual player John Allen, who went on to manage the Cork hurlers to an All-Ireland, in the 1976 Munster final. Cork should have beaten Kerry the same day. Their afternoon was probably summed up by John Allen winning the ball and he's coming in along the end line, going towards the goal and he takes a solo. But just as he takes the tap with his foot, Johno makes this crazy dive and flicks the ball away from him over the end line for a 45 – it was an incredible piece of defending. I was fixated on this.

Tomás and Darragh would be standing over me saying, 'Look, it's time for *The Sunday Game*' or whatever and I'd rewind it one more time and watch the passage of play again while the remote control was being wrestled off me. I used to just marvel in the excellence in defending.

There was another clip I stored in my mental folder; Séamus Moynihan against Oisín McConville in 2000. A ball passes in between the two of them – Séamo reads it to perfection, and Ger Canning provides the soundtrack: 'Here's Oisín McConville, taking on Moynihan.'

It was one-on-one and McConville tried to go inside but was blocked, went outside and found the way blocked too. Oisín didn't even try to go by him in the replay.

I just couldn't get over this. He was like Paul McGrath in Yankee Stadium reading everything, looking as if he had the benefit of the script of the game beforehand. But that's a skill too, and intelligence as much as athleticism.

I remember Mick Lyons, the famous Meath defender, and Jimmy Kerrigan – whose son Paul tortured me years later – was coming through on goal during one of the brilliant Cork–Meath wars.

Jesus, Mick Lyons appears seemingly out of nowhere to make a block. Robbie O'Malley of Meath was another fellow who I thought was excellent and who I studied.

I loved soccer too and growing up as a Man Utd fan in the 1990s I idolised Roy Keane and loved seeing him clatter into the likes of Zidane and Vieira but come away with the ball and drive forward again.

And I went back to those tapes of Páidí and I had this amazing resource on my doorstep throughout my development who'd talk to me in detail about the technicalities of defending at any time.

So, number one, I knew that the position required just all-out defending. Stopping your man, negating your man's influence on the game. You weren't always going to be able to do that because it depended on how well or how poorly you were going midfield, depended on the amount of ball you were coming into. But there were ways and means to train for that too.

For example, if I was training and if I was marking the Gooch and any of Séamo, Darragh, Tomás or Paul Galvin, or Declan O'Sullivan or any of those players got the ball, I knew their first instinct was going to be to kick the ball.

I had to be touch-tight on Gooch or Mike Frank or Donaghy or whoever I was marking. I knew if they got the ball – bang! – this ball is coming.

Gooch and Mike Frank knew the ball was coming too and it gave me a greater level of appreciation for our team. I knew we had good players who could do good things with the ball and kick the ball and that's what the game is about.

Obviously, the systems that have been put in place since have kind of disrupted that, but that's what our game was based on – and moving the ball at speed. And if you were playing in a training session where you were marking the likes of the Gooch, there were nights I'd come home and he might have kicked 1–3 off me or, you know, 2–1 or something like that.

And I'd go home of a Tuesday night and I actually

wouldn't sleep and I'd be like, *Oh my God, I can't wait for Thursday night so that I can go in and try and right the wrongs.*

I'd go in and ask whoever was in charge, 'Throw me in on Gooch there again, just to see can I get the better of him this time.' That's the way it was.

I came home from training one night in Darragh's car and I was gutted, 'Jesus Christ, Gooch got me for 1–3 there tonight.' I was feeling deflated after a tough evening's work.

And Darragh made a good point, which stayed with me thereafter. 'You do realise,' he said, 'you're marking the best forward in the game, so if he's doing that to you, you're also getting the best training in the game? You have to understand that it's a game of backs and forwards. The ball is coming in the whole time. That's not going to happen in a match.'

I could see his theory there and it helped me sleep that night. But, like anyone, I wanted to have that excellence in training where you keep the likes of the Gooch scoreless, which in those games was never really going to happen.

A week after we beat Limerick in the Munster championship – and a couple of weeks out from the provincial decider with Cork – there was an incident in Páidí's pub.

A drink was spilled and suddenly a couple of fights erupted, which would be highly unusual in what is a very well-run family pub. Páidí had to go to court afterwards where he told the judge there was a ratio of nine women to one man in the place at the time.

'It was a very busy night with trainee teachers and Irish language students,' he said. 'I can understand why all the lads came out.'

He added, getting into his stride, that once upon a time girls would come from all over to west Kerry to meet him but now his nephews, who play for Kerry – and were in the bar drinking Lucozade, he said – were the attraction.

The judge dismissed any charges against Páidí. I don't think any of us were in the bar at the time but Páidí wasn't going to let that fact get in the way of a good story.

Early in 2006, myself and Darragh went away to New York to Dara Ó Cinnéide's wedding.

It was during the league and I remember Jack O'Connor said, 'We'll see what way the boys come home; we'll see what kind of shape they're in to see are they kind of like fully with us, are they on board with us? Do they really commit?'

We weren't living like hermits going around Manhattan. We were having a few pints but we weren't dogging it at the same time and I'd say Jack knew that, and we came home and we beat Laois in the semi-final in Killarney. I was full back, Tomás was wing back, Darragh was midfield.

We won by 1–15 to 10 points and that was a strong Kerry team with Murphy, Aidan O'Mahony, myself, Tom Sullivan, Tomás, Moynihan, Mossie Lyons, Dara. You had the likes of Paul Galvin, Fitzmaurice, Sheehan, Gooch, Declan on that team. It was taking shape.

In Páidí's pub there's a lovely little snug that was once assigned to visiting musicians. I sat in there myself many evenings trying to keep up with some of the best around.

Some years before he passed, however, Páidí converted it into a space that now reflects his respect and affection for our neighbours across the border.

Every inch of that cosy corner is covered in pictures of Cork greats like Jimmy Barry-Murphy, Larry Tompkins, Teddy McCarthy, Billy Morgan, Sonia O'Sullivan, Roy Keane and Christy Ring – a murderers' row of Irish sporting greats, all from the Rebel County.

People ask me was Páidí taking the piss with this homage to our rivals. Absolutely not at all. There was huge respect for Cork and the people it produced.

The likes of Billy Morgan and Dr Con, amongst many other opponents from Leeside, are still familiar faces around the bar through the years and the rivalry was always sporting.

Kerry had it over Cork for many years, of course, but the likes of Billy turned that around more than once. I had a rivalry with Cork that was just as keen but less friendly. Maybe those relationships will develop yet.

Throughout my career, I felt that Cork were a serious team, that could beat us on any given day. But I always had confidence that we were, essentially, better. And though they were beating us in Munster, when we got to Croke Park, we had something over them, I thought.

It happened in 2002. Was it a psychological thing for Cork? Or was Croke Park a place where maybe Kerry just thrived? I think a bit of both. Croke Park was a stadium in which our team really enjoyed playing but I don't think Cork were out of their depth there and I think the Dublin team afterwards would vouch for that.

Cork were exceptional during the 2009–11 period and should have won another All-Ireland – whatever *should* means when it comes to sport.

They had players who could hurt us – Graham Canty would tear up the field and get a goal or Nicholas Murphy might dominate in the middle of the field. But we just knew that when the chips were down, our players – Declan O'Sullivan, Paul Galvin, Tomás, Darragh, Gooch, Mike Frank, you name them – these fellas would show up.

In 2006, James Masters kicked 1–6 in the Munster final replay; he absolutely destroyed Mike McCarthy. But when it came to it later in the year, Mike ended up with the Celtic Cross.

I used to generally hold my own against Cork, except for that terrible day out I'd had in the replay the week my dad died. Fionán Murray had kicked three points off me that afternoon on Leeside. Apart from that, I didn't really concede that much.

It was mainly Donncha O'Connor I'd mark over those years. But also, as time went on, Colm O'Neill then became their dangerman and Daniel Goulding. They were all dangerous forwards in various ways.

And then for a while they went with Paul Kerrigan in there and I found his pace a challenge. I liked to think I could cover the ground but he was frightening and I used to have to read the game more to compensate.

The Cork comedian Cornelius O'Sullivan sums up brilliantly what it is to follow the footballers in the Rebel County.

In his video of 'two' Cork supporters – a hurling and football fan respectively – an annoyed Connie wonders why his friend has missed a big championship game.

Timmy explains that he was absent from the hurling because he was knocked down by a car, was badly injured and was on life-support.

'Cork needed you, like, and you weren't there,' Connie tells him, not accepting the excuse.

'What are you talking about?' Timmy replies. 'Sure, I'll see you at the football match tomorrow. Cork are playing above in Limerick.'

His friend is bemused, 'I'd say you got a fair slap of that car alright, boy, because most of the brains have fallen out through your ears. I wouldn't be seen dead at a football game.'

It's scary to see how far Cork football has plummeted.

Kicking a ball against my parents' house in the late 1980s, I imagined myself as Niall Cahalane, Teddy Mc or Larry Tompkins. That team played a swashbuckling, hard-edged brand of football with the charismatic Billy Morgan on the line and the Cork supporters were more than happy to back them.

They were some players – but real men, in the sporting sense. Where have the leaders gone now for Cork? The likes of Brian Hurley and Paul Kerrigan have kept the red flag flying over the past few years but they need more.

One psychological idiosyncrasy of Cork football over the past decade has been a hugely frustrating inability to back up a result. Think back to the Covid years when Mark Keane stunned Kerry with that late goal in the Munster semi-final in an empty Páirc Uí Chaoimh. What a victory, against the head, in a strange, loser-leaves-town championship. One strike and Kerry were gone!

What happens the next day? Cork lose to Tipperary in the Munster final. My God, it's hard for a supporter to hang their hat on a team like that. That sequence is part of a pattern that has defined Cork football for a long time now.

But, in my time, we came up against a proper Rebels outfit.

I always loved going to Páirc Uí Chaoimh. But the same way travelling supporters sometimes complain about how tricky it is to access – we didn't hang around trying to get out of there either.

I loved the old stadium and how tight it was, the atmosphere it brought with the supporters up on top of you – plus the pitch was incredible after they changed it. But trying to negotiate a route up the marina was a nightmare because we'd be stuck on the bus.

In 2006, because there was a minor game on before us, the senior players could only throw their gear bags into the other dressing rooms when the young lads were gone out on the field.

The place is state-of-the-art now, of course, though it came at a price, and it has fantastic facilities. But this was the old ground which contributed to a Cork strike.

The striking Cork players could have called me to address any mediation – I would have told the meeting that trying to pee inside in those dressing rooms was like being inside a phone box. And there were probably only three showers available for a panel of players to share.

But what I loved about Páirc Uí Chaoimh was that you'd come out of the little dressing room and you'd have to go through all the fans in the rat-run under the stands to get out onto the pitch. I really enjoyed running that gauntlet as the two sets of fans stood back and slapped you on the back. It was in slightly better nick than the Colosseum in Rome and there was a gladiatorial feeling to emerging from that warren of tunnels.

When we lost to Cork in the 2006 replay, Jack O'Connor came back into the dressing room and he wanted to rally the troops, get us all together and aligned before we took on the rest of the championship.

When he entered the dressing room, however, some of his players were missing. The trio of Ó Sés were *as láthair*. He was totally demoralised.

'How are we going to win in All-Ireland,' he said, 'if these lads are gone offside? The three boys are probably gone up through the town now, ordering a pint in the Washington Inn before the rest of us have pulled off our boots.'

Jack came out of the stadium, however, climbed onto the team bus and found the three of us waiting in our seats. We were oblivious to any talk going on inside. We'd lost to Cork down the marina – so we just got the hell out of there. And we weren't the only three; there were one or two more sitting patiently on the bus.

We had a proper meeting in the Hayfield Manor where we were having our meal and Séamus Moynihan and Darragh spoke very well. It was clear that the Ó Sés were on board.

A relieved Jack said afterwards that Shakespeare and Julius Caesar came to mind: 'There is a tide in the affairs of men. Which, taken at the flood, leads on to fortune.' Or as Elvis said: 'It's now or never.'

CHAPTER 16

KERRYMEN CAN'T JUMP

Before we played Longford in the qualifiers, Jack asked me after training to hang back. He told me to go in full back and he sent the new guy in the panel in full forward. Kieran Donaghy, a big, untested basketball player could be a secret weapon for Kerry.

Jack kicked a few balls in himself on top of us. What I knew straight away was if it was a long ball over the top, Donaghy was good over his head. But if it was a short ball in front, he was still quick to get out in front.

So now you were marking a fellow who, if you're going to go long or if you're going to go short, you're tested. It was catch-22 for me that evening, and I knew it would be for defences around the country.

'Good stuff, Kieran,' Jack said. 'Go on away there.'

Donaghy trotted in and Jack quizzed me in the middle of the pitch. 'What do you think?'

I said, 'Jesus, he's a serious option. He's deceptively fast. He's good over his head. He can win his own ball. And he'd bring other fellas into play.'

That proved to be the case against Longford. He was excellent and had a hand in most of the good things that Kerry did that day. Now, could he back that up against Armagh?

Kieran brought something completely different to the pitch and what we could do tactically – but just as importantly maybe, he was a breath of fresh air in the dressing room.

He came into training in these boots made by some crowd Nomis. No, me neither.

I remember going into the physio and seeing them and asking, 'Where the fuck did you get these things?' They were massive, size 14, monstrosities. They were chronic.

And he was like, 'Ah, no, man. They're class.'

Then he got a goal against Armagh and he said to me, 'See what I told you, man? I'll have to buy you a pair of Nomis.' He was different.

He brought a whole basketball vibe to a traditional GAA set up. He wore baggy street clothes, had that townie cockiness and went around like Shaquille O'Neal giving high fives to the backroom lads and dishing out these complicated handshakes.

I always said to him, 'Go away with that high-five shite.' But he was excellent and we were delighted to have him.

Donaghy was superb against Armagh. But Darragh too was just on another level; he was incredible and was the reason we beat them.

I enjoyed one of my best days in a Kerry jersey, getting out the field more, allowing me to get on more ball and try to kick a score or two.

I got on the scoresheet when I cut up the field and kicked the ball over the bar by the Hill 16 end.

Later, the ball went up the Hogan Stand side and then the play evolved around the other way towards the Cusack. Tomás first passed it over an Armagh player and I was right in front of the Hill, though I saw Francie Bellew coming.

I said, *I better do something here or else this fella will throw me into the Cusack Stand.*

I dummy soloed with the right on to the left and knocked it over the bar. It was the kind of a move that I was doing all my life in the backyard. I must have pulled that out a thousand times over the years so when I was in that situation in the middle of Croke Park, it just came naturally.

As well as that, it was me just expressing myself as a player and it was lovely to be able to do that in a quarter-final. When something like that comes off in a game as big as that and you're practising it your whole life, you get a real thrill from that.

We knew how good Armagh were. They'd won in 2002 and might well have backed it up a year later if Stevie McDonnell hadn't been denied by Conor Gormley. They were one of the top teams of that era.

But – not to steal a Dublin manager's famous words – we stuck to the process, in that we were kicking long ball in from a diagonal to Donaghy – that was the plan.

And as the years went by, we kind of went away from that and then it was just bombed on top of him, thinking that he was the greatest person of all time, that he could win any type of a ball. It didn't do him any favours. They were the most agricultural kicks you'd ever come across.

But that day Seán O'Sullivan went for a point well into the second half and Donaghy – who had taken lots of physical abuse from Bellew and from other fellas – won the ball. He dropped to his knees and had to battle to get up again.

He still had a bit of work to do and bang – he stuck a goal. You could see from the reaction of him what it meant. He just let it all out.

He apologised after for getting in the keeper's face. I didn't think he should have said sorry but he won the PR battle as well as the fight on the pitch in the end.

It just showed the emotional character that he is and it's part of the reason we as a group appreciated him so much and why the Irish sports fans liked him too.

Darragh played like a man possessed that day and gave one of the great midfield performances.

Armagh may have got the better of us in the 2002 battle but Darragh won the war with every opponent, I would argue, in his career. I felt a huge sense of relief. A weight, which I didn't realise I carried from the disappointment of the 2002 final, was lifted off me.

We hadn't erased that or put anything right; Armagh still won the 2002 All-Ireland. But I'd shown I was a different player now. After the game, Seán Walsh, the Kerry chairman, stuck his head inside the dressing room. RTÉ were looking for a Kerry player.

Seán roared, 'Gentlemen, RTÉ are looking for today's man of the match … Darragh Ó Sé!'

Everyone let up a full-throated cheer and it was a nice gee-up. We felt like a good group. That stands as one of the highlights of my career.

I claimed my second All-Ireland medal when we beat Mayo well in the final again: 4–15 to 3–5. Gooch and Donaghy got 1–2 each, the captain Declan O'Sullivan raised a green flag and my friend Eoin Brosnan got on to score a goal too.

Moving Donaghy to full forward for the Longford game

was a masterstroke from Jack and Kieran helped get us back up the Hogan Stand steps. It made him as a player and changed our team for the better.

CHAPTER 17

FOOTBALLER OF THE YEAR

Barry John Keane popped into my place recently to pick up my young lad Tadhg to take him to basketball with his son, Leo.

As they were packing up, he said to me, 'C'mere, I watched the 2005 final against Tyrone there the other night. My God,' he said, 'we gave some ball away.'

He was right and we left that one after us. But the seeds of my personal success in 2007 started that year, I think.

Jack O'Connor wrote a lot of things in his book *Keys to the Kingdom* – including that I would have won Footballer of the Year in 2005 if we had got over the line. I don't know about that at all but I was hitting my straps and felt a key member of the team.

I remember in that final I was right in front of the goal

in the Davin End and I got the ball and I dummy soloed a fella. It was a bit like the point I got against Armagh in the 2006 quarter-final.

I threw it on to the right leg again, dummy with the right and instead of going with the in step, I went to the outside of the right boot and it just scuffled off my leg. It was a percentage shot, but right in front of the post. It should have been a point all day long and I'd say I would have been in the conversation for an All Star had I got it. Not that it's about that.

But it shows the margins – Jack saying I should've got the top individual award and I ended up without even an All Star.

That's how fickle these things are, and at the end of the day, they're not really that important. Getting over the line, winning All-Irelands, that's what matters.

I knew from 2005 that I was at the level that I needed to be at finally, after a good 2004, and the curve was heading in the right direction. I was given the fireman role – cutting out the danger, putting out fires – more so from 2006.

After we won the All-Ireland in 2006, we were above, sitting down having a drink in a lounge in Croke Park and the TV broadcast was on. We were relaxing, chatting amongst ourselves and half watching the programme as players were being interviewed.

The panel were picking their team of the year and Tony Davis said, 'Ah sure look, the No 2 position is nailed on,' in reference to me. It clearly meant something to me, even then, if it sticks in my mind.

I know it gave me satisfaction that people were seemingly seeing what Jack was seeing and though getting over the line and winning the All-Ireland was the primary goal, people showing appreciation was nice, at that stage of my career.

Having said that, surrounded by my family and teammates, there was no chance of me getting carried away. I was ball hopping with Páidí in the weeks afterwards, about how we were catching up with him when it came to All-Ireland medals.

'Come back to me when you need two hands to count yours,' he replied quickly.

There's a phrase in Irish – a *seanfhocail* – and it was something that I made my mantra in my early days in a Kerry jersey and beyond it: '*An té nach bhfuil láidir ní foláir dó a bheith glic* [He who isn't strong needs to be clever].'

That journey to being Footballer of the Year had begun in my parents' back garden kicking ball with my brothers. I was the smallest, of course, but learned to nip in and get the ball away or make a block – I made a career out of it. If I was marking a player who was a bit stronger, I'd wait for them to take their solo and get a hand in. I'd try to be cute and flick it away. Or if they were about to shoot, I'd get down on that ball and block it.

Back in the day when there were four of us in the crowded

back garden and I wasn't strong enough to take on Tomás or Darragh or Fergal, I'd be able to block. Sometimes I'd get a boot to the head and would end up crying at the kitchen table.

But eventually, I ended up adept at blocking. And I liked being able to pull it off. Like most houses throughout the country, we had a copy of *Kerry's Golden Years* on VHS and we absolutely wore it out. I, of course, took in the great scores, the high fielding and performance of my uncle Páidí but even then, I made sure to note the shouldering of Paudie Lynch.

He often pulled a great trick of going in for a shoulder or checking and leaving the player go past by pulling the hand-brake.

I'd need every trick in my book against Monaghan. It's a game we should have lost.

I was on Tommy Freeman who was red hot. We were really struggling and Freeman kicked two points off me, one off the right and one off the left. Monaghan had smothered us all afternoon with their impressive brand of physicality.

And there were times in that game when it was tough trying to keep our head above water. They were really coming after us and that game went down the stretch. The turning point came with Freeman through and ready to pull the trigger, as they led by a point. A goal would send us out of the championship.

I was back in that back garden. It was a two v. one situation but I hedged my bets, committing to other players, until the last moment when I dove in and got a two-handed block down at Freeman's bootlaces.

As somebody put it lately, it wasn't the winning of the game, but it was more certainly the saving of the game, because if that goal had gone in, we would have lost the game.

At half time we were in disarray but Darragh stood in the centre of the dressing room and got a hold of us – calming the room and leading us once again.

We won by a point: 1–12 to 1–11 and it was the hardest game we played all year, without a shadow of a doubt.

When Jack O'Connor left after the 2006 All-Ireland, Pat O'Shea came in as the new manager.

He may have only been there for a couple of years in the end, but he'd have a powerful impact on my career. And we had a connection that went back a long time.

When I was around eight or nine years old, it was the time when coaches started going to schools, the GDAs or games development administrators, as they call them. Pat O'Shea was the first GDA that ever came to my school, Cill Mhic an Domhnaigh just a mile from the house. He brought in a big bulging bag of balls, seven or eight O'Neill's footballs. Our eyes lit up.

This was a small country school with 26 pupils in total

maybe. Pat brought us out the back – the entire student body – and put us through our very first drill.

Soloing the ball on the right, turning straight onto the left, soloing the ball at the left, soloing at the right, soloing at the left, soloing at the right. He spent around a half hour with us and he gathered up his balls and said, 'Right, I'll come back next week.'

Jesus, we were counting the hours for him to return, but he did. All we wanted was to have improved at that drill in the meantime. I had it perfected from the repetition in my parents' garden. Little did I realise that I was working on my left leg, something that I had not really done as a boy.

Now I see my kids and they start at U7s. The first bit of football we had was U12s. But I was developing the skillset that most fellas wouldn't have had because of the work that I was putting in.

Obviously, my older brothers were a huge influence and my uncles and dad. But Pat was important at that age in my development. It's fair to say he's the best coach that I ever had in teaching the simple basics of the game.

Later, when Pat was appointed Kerry boss, he tried to coach me in how to be a footballer. He handed me a book. I looked at the cover with Michael Jordan on it – a biography of the great Chicago Bulls player – and I asked Pat why this was something I should spend my time on.

Like any sports-mad kid in the 1990s I'd consumed as

much Jordan as I could, in the days without cable television and the internet – but I didn't immediately realise why being 'Like Mike' would help Kerry. What could we learn in Kerry from the Bulls?

Pat explained that Jordan was not only the greatest talent, but he was also the greatest because every time he went to a game, whatever game he was playing, he said to himself, *There's somebody that's watching me for the very first time and I want to let them know how good I am and then walk away from this game knowing they've seen greatness, knowing they've seen Michael Jordan.*

I don't think Pat was suggesting I was Michael Jordan. What I took from it was every day you go all-in playing. He wanted us to be the best version of ourselves every day.

I'm not sure if I even read the whole book in the end but I understood the message that Pat was trying to pass on to me. I thought it was a clever way of doing it and I committed to doubling down on my efforts for Kerry.

And it was no coincidence that that was probably my best year; the fact that I was lucky enough to get the player of the year shows that.

But then all the years that I played after that, everything was about just performing, performing, performing and everything that I did led to performing, be it in training, the gym, sleeping, everything just lent itself to performing on the field. And if you didn't show up, you'd ask yourself questions, *Why? What happened there? Was there something that you didn't do right? Were you maybe doing too much travelling, not enough sleep, not enough eating* or whatever it was. Pat brought that sense of professionalism to my game that hadn't been there in the past.

Pat always wanted his players to be the best that they could be and that was always the goal for me. Often it didn't happen and then you'd come back playing club football. The club players would want to be better because they were playing against county players and would improve their performance as a result. So you really had to be tuned in.

We had Dublin in the All-Ireland semi-final and I was marking my old pal, Alan Brogan.

I grew up on the Kerry–Dublin rivalry, watching videos of the great Kerry teams taking on Heffo's Army all up through the years. Those games took on a life of their own and I was one of those players who really took energy from the colosseum that Croke Park became.

The noise that came off the Hill when you were playing in front of it was insane. And I'd consciously try to feed off it. It would be a sea of colour – blue – with a wall of noise rolling towards you. I'd still be able to pick out little funny lines, someone calling us culchies and the rest.

But I liked it and would always use that to my advantage. I always say that to any team I'm coaching. It may not be a full Croke Park against Dublin, but whatever situation you're in, just feed off that.

Take that negativity and turn it to your advantage. It was a cauldron and it was where we wanted to be. At the same time, it brought practical challenges. Tomás might have been 15 yards outside me and I'd be roaring at him at the top of my voice – a simple instruction – shouting at him and he couldn't hear me.

There were still moments where you'd think, *How cool is this that we're here* and Darragh might be out to field in front of us, but the grass beneath us is the famous Croke Park pitch and not the lawn that hugs my homeplace.

But you'd be trying to communicate with your teammates and you can understand why the role of the runner was vital because just trying to get heard was hard enough, even at club level. Can you imagine 82,000 people in Croke Park and a large section of them instructing you to go back to the bog? It's impossible.

The pace and intensity of those games was ferocious.

The first one really that I noticed was our 2006 quarter-final. That game was at a pace that we'd never played it before. Those were huge eye openers and certainly those Dublin teams got so strong afterwards. It's satisfying to look back in my career and be able to say, 'Hold on a second, no, I have a good, decent enough record against them.'

It was the same that day. Dublin put it up to us and it was a tough game. They came at us and they fed on the strength from the Hill. But we always felt we had enough for them.

The team was strong: Tom O'Sullivan and myself in the full back line; Tomás and Aidan O'Mahony in the half back line; Darragh and Séamus Scanlan in the middle of the field; Declan and Paul Galvin and Brossie and then Gooch and Donaghy and Bryan Sheehan in full forward.

At one stage I came over the ball and tore off down the side of the Hogan Stand, ended up passing it to Donaghy, who gave it to Galvin – bang, over the bar.

I met Páidí afterwards for a pint and he was in great form. He caught me and said, 'Jesus, when I saw you coming down the side of the Hogan Stand, I jumped up out of my seat.' He shook his head, 'I jumped up in the air with excitement.'

It was great to hear those kinds of stories and I got a huge satisfaction in giving Páidí those moments. Our father wasn't with us anymore and not in the seat he should have been, enjoying our performances. But it was great that Páidí and my uncle Tom still had that interest for us.

I was marking my friend Alan Brogan. We'd been pally from the first day we met in Maynooth.

I'd walked into a trial for the team there, and I'd say no one knew who I was, which suited me fine.

I'd torn into Brogan and afterwards he'd been asking me who I was and where I was from.

Afterwards, I'd been heading into the city and he'd rolled down the window of his mother's car and offered me a lift. His mom, Marie – a Keane-Stack from Kerry – was so good to me afterwards.

Alan was the main threat on that team in 2007, and at one stage – I'm not sure what happened – a bit of a shemozzle broke out at half time.

As we walked towards the dressing room, Brogan was quick to hold up two fingers and remind me of his tally. 'Two points, Marc,' he says. 'Two points, two points!' roaring at me, and we go in at half time.

I was completely bemused and had to laugh. But yeah, that was Alan – he was a player who played with his heart.

I have fond memories of him taking on the Aussies in 2006 and 2008. Christ, I even remember him back as far as 2002 when we were in college. We'd been on a Sigerson trip and the evening had ended up with Alan rolling around the floor of a chipper at two in the morning with some lad.

I reminded him of it recently and he said, 'Wooly Parkinson started that.' But that was the type of a fella Alan was; he wasn't going to back down from anything and I love that about him.

He's a great character and we've always remained close since, and that's something that I've taken from those games against the Dubs.

I went up to Dublin for his 40th and was at his wedding

and that's something special about the GAA – you always have those friendships. I'm still good buddies with the likes of Declan Lally, Barry Cahill, Alan's brother Bernard.

After big games, Bernard and Alan would be the first fellas you'd seek out – whatever way the result went.

I'd heard a story about one evening in Kruger's public house in Dunquin in October 1981. Páidí had put the receiver down after he'd taken in the information and made his way back towards his homeplace in Ard an Bhóthair. Beatrice suspected her son had come with news and when she detected the start of a smile behind his poker face, she felt relief that it was positive.

'Out with it,' she'd said.

'I'll be needing a tux,' Páidí had said. He'd won his first All Star, according to a source. The newspapers confirmed the news officially the following morning. For us Ó Sés it was the first of 17 of the accolades.

We blitzed Cork in the final. Job done again.

At the All Stars dinner I was having a bottle of beer in a corner with Gooch and Declan O'Sullivan, two of the guys who were candidates for Footballer of the Year, along with me. Either of them would have been deserving winners.

One of the organisers of the night approached us and said, 'Marc, you're going to win Footballer of the Year tonight.' I'd be a fool or a liar to say I wasn't proud. I was so proud.

Obviously, you reflect on what the honour means and who's won before you, the people who helped you achieve it and those who aren't around to share the evening with you.

But I'll be honest, I was so embarrassed at the same time. Because Declan was awesome that year. Gooch was awesome that year. I felt a small bit like a fraud getting that award ahead of the two of them, in particular.

And I know people might laugh at that or not understand it or even suspect this is false modesty. But that's the way I was feeling. Analyse that.

Somebody said to me that night that I'd broken new territory. He meant a Footballer of the Year coming from corner back – Robbie O'Malley was the only other one to do that, in 1988. In previous years my teammates like Tomás, Kieran Donaghy and Paul Galvin had won it. Before that, superb players like Peter Canavan, Maurice Fitzgerald and Trevor Giles had earned the accolade.

So that gave me a bit of pride – I love defending and it was great to represent that craft.

But I thought Declan and Colm were better than me that year and though I was nominated I was fairly relaxed about the evening. I honestly never contemplated that me winning was a real possibility. One of the two lads would have been the more obvious choice.

That embarrassment was mixed with the pride as well, especially when I thought of An Ghaeltacht, Mícheál Ó Sé, Liam Ó Rócháin, Tom Ó Cruadhlaoich, my parents and family, my place.

There is that pride in it for the people that helped you earn this. There's pride there for that.

Tomás had won it before me. Darragh should have won it twice before me in 2002 and 2006.

It was a blur thereafter but I remember the three of us brothers being interviewed by Ger Canning and I had always loved him as a commentator and grew up watching games and listening to him.

And then you find yourself up in front of your peers, holding a piece of hardware, being interviewed by this man. It was a lovely moment that the three of us were up there and we were the first three brothers who had won All Stars together.

I think people kind of gloss over that fact. It was nice winning the player of the year, but it was also lovely that the three of us got All Stars on the one night.

No matter whatever happens, I always go back to An Ghaeltacht's football field at Gallarus. And when I go into the clubhouse, I see that photograph of the three of us with our monkey suits on and the All Stars, that's a lovely moment.

I thought too of the doubts I had as a young player growing up in the long shadow of my brothers and uncle, worried that I wouldn't hold up my part of the bargain and be known as a lad who was better at getting a tune out of an accordion than kicking ball.

When Mikey Sheehy was one of Éamonn Fitzmaurice's selectors, he would often tell me, 'You'll win Footballer of the Year before your career is over.' A smart man, maybe he picked up on the fact that hearing that would be good for me. I never believed him.

After the ceremony in 2007, my phone pinged with a text from Mikey. 'What did I tell you?' he wrote.

The three of us brothers winning All Stars together on the night I was awarded the top individual honour was a memorable moment and a great achievement for our family, but I can't say it was a surprise – thanks to our uncle.

On a dark December evening in 2007, Páidí, standing behind the bar at Ard an Bhóthair, put down the phone and made an announcement to those sitting in the pub. It was just minutes after the All Stars selection committee had broken up from their meeting in the Westbury Hotel off Grafton Street. He let everyone know us three brothers would be honoured some few days later at the All Stars banquet. He always had his source in the room.

CHAPTER 18

ONCE UPON A TIME IN THE WEST

Cork eventually got their All-Ireland, which they deserved, in 2010.

I was in college, in CIT, with the likes of Graham Canty, Derek Kavanagh, some more of the lads. I got on well with them at the time but didn't really mingle with them afterwards and keep up the friendship.

Am I friends with any of the Cork players now? No, not really. But it wouldn't be out of any kind of them-and-us sort of thing. That wouldn't be it.

In fact, I'm still good friends with teammates from my days later in Maynooth. I kept up all those friendships because I was there longer. I was only in Cork for a year or so. And maybe it's different now with social media and seminars that the players' union organises and things like that – players now seem to be more familiar with each other, for better or worse.

The morning after the 2007 All-Ireland final, I woke up with a well-earned hangover and went in search of a cure. I had a hunch I'd find my brothers and some teammates in O'Brien's on Leeson Street.

I swung open the door to this lovely, traditional little pub and strode inside with the swagger of a man who was celebrating an All-Ireland final victory. Rather than find my teammates propping up the bar, however, I walked into, what seemed like, the entire Cork panel, who were quietly having a drink.

It was like a western when the cowboy walks into the wrong hostelry, the piano music stops and all eyes are on the stranger as he approaches the bartender. I immediately felt like a right eejit but quickly made the calculation that I couldn't just turn around now and walk out.

I got to the counter, sheepishly called a pint and realised it was literally me, the barman and the Cork panel, all in their suits, inside in this pub. I just wanted the ground to swallow me up and resolved to drink the beer up quickly.

But in fairness to Donncha O'Connor, who I was marking the previous day, he soon came over, tapped me on the back and shook my hand. The music seemed to start again and, to my mind, people got back to their conversations.

'Jesus Christ, Donncha,' I said, 'I was actually looking for my two brothers. I didn't come in here to lord anything over anyone. I wasn't expecting to come in here and see ye. I certainly wasn't gloating.'

But he knew that and was very gracious. We had a nice chat and I appreciated how decent he was on behalf of his team. He could have stayed sitting down and they could have made a bit of a prick out of me.

But in fairness, he didn't and I always respected him for that.

I'd say I still put the pint away in three sups and made my excuses, but I never forgot Donncha offering me his hand.

Myself and him had great battles on the field; he would have kicked a couple of scores, but obviously from a Kerry point of view, Jack O'Connor and later Pat O'Shea would have known that I could keep him relatively quiet.

We certainly felt he was Cork's dangerman over those years, and if we could keep him somewhat subdued, we were doing a good day's work.

Plus, Donncha was on the border there – Ballydesmond. And you look at anyone who lives on the border and that … is hatred the right word? That rivalry is way more passionate and comes through when you're on the border.

I'll never forget, in 2009, Millstreet of Cork were playing Kerry's Rathmore, who are ironically red and white, and from just over the other side of the county bounds.

The Sam Maguire was there and it was an opportunity for these two young teams – maybe they were U12s – to entertain this big crowd. Never in my life did I hear the likes of the chat from the players: 'Ye'll never fucking have this' and stuff like that.

I was saying, 'What's going on here?' It was just mental stuff. But it just shows you the intensity of the rivalry there.

But what makes me sad is the fact that that's not there at all anymore. I don't think Kerry and Cork have a rivalry now. It'd be better for the game, and Kerry, if Cork were better. Páidí has that snug filled with Rebel County heroes because his team were pushed on by Cork.

Later, our team was winning All-Irelands when Cork were good; Cork won an All-Ireland when we were good.

I think we brought out the best in each other; steel sharpens steel. But that rivalry is definitely a thing of the past.

CHAPTER 19

SEEING RED

I may be colour blind, but I had no problem seeing red over the course of my career.

During his career, Páidí played the game at full throttle and was physical but his disciplinary record shows he wasn't a dirty player. I think many people did have the wrong image of him, however.

He was described by Owen McCrohan in a great book about Mick O'Dwyer as having 'about as much refinement as a broken bottle and whenever he pulled on a jersey he looked as endearing as a bulldog.' Harsh.

A punch he threw in 1975 probably cost him a few All Stars awards – I know he thought as much.

If it happened now, the incident would be super viral within seconds and one can only imagine what the various pundits would say. Even though it happened a half century ago, the encounter with Cork's Dinny Allen is a YouTube staple.

Allen, who'd go on to skipper Cork to an All-Ireland in 1989, was part of the Rebels' team taking on Kerry in the Munster final of 1975. Billy Morgan would save a penalty from Mikey Sheehy and Kingdom keeper Paud O'Mahony would deny Jimmy Barry-Murphy from a penalty kick.

But the game is remembered for Allen v. Ó Sé.

Páidí's version of the tussle, with a man he later regarded as a friend, started when the Nemo man kicked a point. Allen, Páidí said, turned to him and said, 'They'll be taking you off soon.'

'If they are, you'll be coming with me,' was Páidí's reply.

Moments later, when Allen gains possession, Páidí gives him a little dunt in the ribs; then Allen swings back his elbow and inadvertently catches Páidí flush in the jaw. A stunned Páidí takes a moment to assess the damage and then delivers a left fist to Allen that floors him. Adding to the slapstick, referee John Moloney arrives on the scene, but his feet go from under him.

By the time he was upright again, the two players had cooled down. He spoke to them and they shook hands and moved on. Neither player was sanctioned and the flare-up was barely mentioned in the papers the following day. There's a nice picture of Allen in the snug in Páidí's bar still.

At half time against Cork in 2008, Joe Brolly and Colm O'Rourke said there's no way Kerry can get beaten here. We showed them.

I was Footballer of the Year and trying again to reach the heights that I'd set for myself and keep going. But we got to the Munster final in Páirc Uí Chaoimh and I was sent off and Darragh was sent off. The two of us were sitting and left looking at each other and saying, 'What the hell just happened there?'

I remember the moment that got me dismissed so vividly. There are moments that stand out in your life. It's the same on the football pitch.

The underfoot conditions were shocking and the ball came down the sideline. Cork kicked the ball out of defence, and I could see it coming. I read it and darted towards the sideline, as I saw Seán O'Brien coming like a train towards me.

Looking to brace myself, I went down on the ball but my feet went flying from under me and bang – I made contact with Seán's head.

I hopped up, turned to the referee, Derek Fahy, and I said, 'There's no way that's a red card.'

Nicholas Murphy had been sent off and I think he was trying to even things up a small bit. 'No,' he says, 'you're going.'

I thought it was a disgraceful decision and made that clear, but I went off towards Pat O'Shea on the sideline. After taking some advice, I had to go up to Croke Park afterwards with Jerome Conway, the Kerry chairman at the time, to talk about the incident in front of the Central Competitions Control Committee.

We all watched the incident on a screen and like a jockey in a steward's enquiry, I had to articulate what I thought happened and make my case. It was a bit like Eamon Dunphy and Johnny Giles talking over match footage: 'Can you hold it there?'

I was advised before going in, 'Don't say "shoulder".' The term was 'high side to side charge' and I was coached on what the exact words should be by an expert. He was a Tyrone man, ironically enough.

I met the man in Croke Park that day and it was clear he was an encyclopaedia on the rulebook and the use of legalese in the context of these court settings. I said my piece in the meeting and told them that as I'm about to go for the ball, you can see my feet skid along the wet pitch, so I braced myself to protect myself.

I wasn't sure if they were convinced but after the meeting, Jerome got a phone call as we were going through the toll on the way home. I was exonerated and free to play the next game.

Later, in 2011, we played the Dubs in a National League game and I got cited afterwards for an incident in injury time with Eoghan O'Gara.

While Bryan Sheehan was preparing to take a free kick, the two of us became entangled and there was a head-to-head moment that was described as a headbutt. But it wasn't really.

Nevertheless, we both got done and were looking at long

bans. Barry John Keane had already picked up a long suspension for a similar incident against Cork, and the year previously Tomás and Paul Galvin were sitting out for lengthy stretches.

But in fairness to O'Gara, he and Pat Gilroy rang me that week and said, 'Look, we'll take the hit for this. We'll exonerate you.'

I appreciated it; it was very fair. But I still ended up with three or four weeks. You win some, lose some.

CHAPTER 20

LAST ORDERS?

Jack announced to the dressing room at half time in the qualifier against Sligo in 2009 that I was coming off.

What the fuck is this, I thought, before things spiralled.

The lads went out and managed to get an unconvincing victory but it looked a long way back to the steps of the Hogan Stand in the days afterwards. We were a squad divided and my relationship with Jack – such as it was – never fully recovered.

After defeat to Cork in the Munster championship, we hosted Sligo and I was marking a tricky corner forward, David Kelly. He was the type of player I hated seeing coming towards me – a small guy in stature but lots of pace and plenty of skill.

I'd honestly much prefer to mark someone like David Clifford – who'll go down as one of the true greats of the game – rather than a guy like Kelly. I'd take my chances in a battle there rather than a Darragh Canavan or his brother Ruairí because those jinky players, I used to find them a headache. And this man, Kelly, from Sligo was like that.

I wasn't playing well in the first half and he got a goal off me and then a point. I was wearing these moulded boots and was slipping all over the place and could not get into the game.

I thought, I'll get in at half time, regroup, change the footwear and we'll go again and put it right. But I'd end up changing into my civvies and shoes.

Éamonn Fitzmaurice, who was a selector with Jack O'Connor at the time, came over to me and said, 'We're gonna switch you.' I was a bit pissed off at the decision because I said, 'Come on, I fancy my chances. I'll get on top of him in the end. I struggled in the first half, but *I will* get on top of him.' I'd be stubborn that way.

But he said, 'Look, no, we're going to put you on the other side.'

I was slightly put out but I said, 'Look, fair enough so if that's the case, but I would love to give him another crack in the second half to get it right.' Anyway, I knew what was happening at least and started to refocus on the new challenge and figure out who was on the other side.

A couple of minutes later, Jack came in to address the panel. He said, 'We're making one change there: we're taking off Marc Ó Sé and bringing on Pádraig Reidy.'

What the fuck is this? I'm thinking.

Fitzmaurice had only a couple of minutes earlier said that I was switching corners. Now I was hooked at half time. I couldn't get my head around it.

When you're subbed off, a player would normally go back out to the dugout and watch from there but by the time I got dressed, the lads had gone out and I decided to head up to the pavilion and watch from that vantage, fuming silently.

I had a good view of Diarmuid Murphy saving a penalty and we got out of jail. As soon as the whistle went, I was out the door.

I hopped in the car and edged out the gate and up the street, where supporters were coming out of the pitch. Some of them would see me, look twice and ask how I got out so quickly. I wasn't in the mood to stick around.

The following week we were to play Antrim in the next round of qualifiers so it should have been all about recovery and preparation for that knockout All-Ireland tie.

In all honesty though I just thought, *Fuck it.*

That day, a Saturday, a buddy of ours, Mikey Sheehy Jr, married his bride Suzanne in the Skellig Hotel in Dingle. Myself and Tomás were going back west anyway and we said we'd pop in to congratulate the newlyweds.

I was fairly pissed off and, though it was the wrong thing to do, I had a few pints at the reception amongst friends.

That few pints led to a few more pints, however. It was nothing at all crazy but not something that should be happening at that stage of the season.

The following day, there were a few buddies around from Birmingham, the Moriartys – great Kerry supporters and people who have always been great to us.

They'd killed three birds with one stone that weekend. They went to the wedding. They went to the game. And the following day they were back in Páidí's, and myself and Tomás said, 'Sure look, we'll have one with them.'

Before we knew it, we were after the gallon. This is where I took the show off the road and called it a day. Others might have knocked another bit out of it.

And the Gooch was unwinding quietly in Killarney. Every fella was ducking and diving to blow off a little steam between these two games. It says a lot about the mood.

The following day, I was fairly shook after a couple of days on the beer and I was in the car when the phone rang. The name flashed up in front of me: Jack O'Connor.

Jesus, don't answer that, I said to myself as I tried to get my story straight.

It transpired that Tomás and the Gooch had been rumbled and had already come clean. Jack rang again and I picked up.

'Marc, you were drinking.' It was a statement, rather than a question.

I said, 'Jesus, no, Jack. I wasn't.' I was shaking inside in the car with porter coming out of me.

'No, Marc, you were drinking. You know you were. You were spotted.'

I doubled down.

'Jack, I wasn't drinking at all.'

'Marc, a friend of mine saw you inside in Páidí's and you were drinking.'

I said, 'Jack, you put that fella in front of me and I'll call him a liar. I wasn't drinking.'

And he said, 'Don't be talking like that. You know you were.'

'I wasn't. I wasn't.'

We played out a stalemate. Later, he came at me a second time in training and I denied everything high up and low down again.

Ger O'Keeffe, who was a selector, was doing a bit of detective work in Tralee meanwhile and he was deadly. He was like the T1000 in *Terminator* – wouldn't give up the chase at all. He kept asking fellas were the Ó Sés drinking with you and we surmised he nearly had a photofit and Wanted posters made up. 'Have you seen this man ordering a stout?'

This is the craic that was going on and it was funny in a way, but at the time it wasn't funny at all. At the time we were completely stressed because the chances were we'd be dropped.

We were in the wrong. But why was this crusade going

on? I think they wanted to blame someone for the performances, which were poor. Again, we were obviously completely in the wrong – first for drinking, and it's not great then having to lie. I said, 'We need to be on the field to help this side win an All-Ireland.'

We were sticking to my story no matter what. Jack called a team meeting.

You know those images that go around of a fella getting out the popcorn when there's a bit of drama? Very appropriate for this episode.

I was often in meetings as a younger player, when I was kind of peripheral, and though these showdowns can be tense or even painful, they're very entertaining too.

In this one, we were at the centre. Mike Quirke was put in charge of the session for whatever reason. Jack felt he had to be at a remove perhaps. At this time, Gooch and Tomás had ended up on the front page of national newspapers for the crime of having a drink. How did the news get out of the camp that Kerry players were drinking?

Especially in that context, we weren't about to admit to management or anyone that we had stepped outside the rules too. Before long, someone asked me directly, 'Marc, were you drinking?'

'No,' I said. 'I was inside in Páidí's and I had a bowl of soup and a sandwich.'

The euphemism became the punchline in jokes from the

boys afterwards and 'soup and a sandwich' became shorthand amongst us for a couple of pints.

'Did you have a few bowls of soup over the weekend?'

'My God, you look like you overdid the soup and sandwiches last night …'

Mike Quirke had a thankless job and Darragh, who evidently thought attack was the best form of defence, asked him, 'What the fuck are you doing chairing this meeting?'

We settled in.

A few people chipped in from the floor saying stuff like, 'Look, if there were more lads out on the beer than Tomás and the Gooch, put your hands up.'

Paul Galvin, who is a great friend of mine and was an unbelievable player for Kerry, said, 'Jesus, look lads if ye were out just put your hands up.' Darragh reminded Paul his discipline issues had meant he hadn't been around for much of the previous year.

Paul, a Footballer of the Year, was totally taken aback. And you can see why – but he shrugged it off in the end. It was two of our leaders thrashing it out.

The atmosphere was tense and a few minutes later Tadhg Kennelly, back for the year from his AFL career, started off saying something and Darragh cut him off saying, 'Jesus Christ, will you pipe down? You're only home a wet week and you're talking like you know what's going on.'

The funny thing was, that pair were great friends and there was plenty of mutual respect.

It was tense and I was keeping the head down. I felt I was wronged by Jack in that game. Two wrongs don't make a right and I'll put my hands up now. I was offside.

If I was a manager now and I took a player off and he felt he was wronged, I'd hope that the player would come to me directly and call me out, whereas I left at full time, went back to Dingle and had a pint. That wasn't right and I totally agree with that. And as I've moved into coaching, I've earned a new perspective and can see more clearly from Jack's point of view.

One thing I've never done as a manager is put in these drinking bans or mad contracts. Close to an important game, I'd remind a group of players to mind their bodies. But I would never say to a group of adults, who are committing to this thing voluntarily, you can't have a glass of wine with a meal or a pint.

After a good while in the meeting, someone said, 'Look, lads, we're getting nowhere,' and the thing ran out of gas.

As fellas started getting out of their chairs, however, Darragh said, 'Hang on a minute now, lads. As far as I'm concerned, this meeting is over, but I want you all to have one quick look at these two fellas inside here.' He pointed at Tomás and Colm, looking sheepish.

'Have a look at Gooch,' he said. 'And have a look at Tomás. I can tell you every single person inside here would not have three, four, five All-Ireland medals, only for those men.'

There was a pause. 'Meeting over,' he said. You could hear a pin drop, and then everyone left. That was Darragh. He was a leader. Now we needed to come down off the moral high ground and do it on the pitch.

CHAPTER 21

FROM BÍN BÁN TO CROKE PARK

I was preparing in midweek by swimming off Bín Bán Strand near Dingle, in the days before the 2009 All-Ireland final.

I was living in the town at the time and paying a visit to the beach was something I often did. I really appreciated the benefit from the seawater and our physios always reminded us how valuable it was to us.

It helped me get the body, and the mind, right in those weeks. Every evening when we were in training, I'd go for a dip afterwards. In the morning-time, I'd go into salt water and I'd meet these two older fellas, Jimmy Flannery and Martin Scanlan, who's passed away since.

It was a social thing too that I enjoyed and Bín Bán, not

too far away from where Mícheál Ó Muircheartaigh came from, was the ideal spot for me.

I was with Jimmy and Martin and my friend, Mícheál Ó Sé Jr in the water when loud screaming prompted us to look up to the cliffs. Two girls had been sitting up there, relaxing and looking out to the sea on what was a beautiful morning. It was apparent one of the girls had slipped down the cliff face and was in trouble. She was trying to hang on at the top of a high drop.

Myself and Mícheál naturally rushed out of the water and made our way up the cliff. I leant over the side, caught her hand and tried to pull her in while Mícheál kept a hold of my legs.

I looked past this poor girl down what was a 40-foot drop, if not even more, below. I tightened my grip and tried to reassure her that we'd get her to safety but we couldn't make any progress in pulling her up.

I lost my grip and she fell. To this day I can still hear the screams and the sounds of that fall.

In a panic, we rushed to the bottom but she was in a very bad way, the poor girl, and an ambulance arrived 20 minutes or so later. We learned afterwards that she was called Maria Philips, from England. She died sometime later in hospital.

It was devastating and I often think about that evening now – especially when out at somewhere beautiful but wild like Coumeenoole beach with our kids. I find myself catching them tight and keeping them closer.

That was the Wednesday before the All-Ireland – but I went into training and up to Dublin later in the week and I didn't mention it to anyone. Maybe it's a male thing and I needed some help in talking it out. Or perhaps it's the selfishness of the athlete – I was able to just compartmentalise that traumatic event until I had the capacity to deal with it, if I ever did. I don't want to sound like a cold-hearted person saying that. But I was able to park it and solely focus on the game and the challenge Cork would bring.

And in fact, football was a comfort and a release. I just needed to worry about Donncha O'Connor and how I was going to try to stop him. I was very happy to have that to concentrate on.

You talk about trust between a player and manager. There was none at that stage between me and Jack. For him to lecture me about the group was hard to take. (When I read about Roy Keane being triggered by Carlos Queiroz talking about loyalty, after his return from Real Madrid, it resonated.)

When he came back to manage us the second time things were different. In the intervening time he'd written his book *Keys to the Kingdom* and brought it out days before the Munster final in 2007.

That was poor timing. If he cared about how it would affect his former players, he would have held fire rather than make our job a lot harder by creating this circus.

There was plenty of stuff in the book about the internal workings of our group. There was lots more he left out I'm sure, but as a *Kerryman* newspaper editorial put it: 'there is as much talk about some of the content of the book as there is about Kerry's prospects on Sunday'.

He was under pressure and had to explain parts about being reimbursed by the county board for expenses but more interestingly to me, it had passages about how the Ó Sés were hard to handle.

I totally disagreed then and now. I think we were actually very easy to handle because all we wanted to do was play football. I thought that it was one thing to tell tales out of school about your former players. It's another then to bring it out while your county is preparing for a Munster final. Don't get me wrong, Jack said some really complimentary stuff as well but that inference that we were hard to handle didn't sit easily with me.

While Cork were preparing to have a pop at us, we spent the week answering questions about *Keys to the Kingdom*.

It was Pat O'Shea's first year in charge. The publication and its timing were mentioned in a team meeting and it was frowned upon when it was brought up. But we left it at that.

Later, when Jack came back in again, that trust that's

required between a player and a manager was diminished. He returned, having written the book and talked about players who would have won him All-Irelands, like that.

To speak like that about us and say the Ó Sés were 'hard to handle' was disrespectful, because at the end of the day, all we ever wanted to do was help Kerry to win.

And you don't have to take my word for it. There are loads of examples around the country in recent modern GAA history of player power like in Mayo or strikes like in Cork. There was never any issue in Kerry. All we wanted to do was get on with playing.

When Jack came in after Páidí, we didn't derail things or make a huge fuss. We just continued on.

In 2009, we were wrong to pull up a bar stool after the Sligo game. But we also thought that situation wasn't handled right at all. For that to be in the front page of national newspapers? That didn't need to happen and I look back now on that time and I'm glad that I didn't put my hand up and confess.

Any time I get the opportunity to talk about it now, I say, 'Of course I was offside and it was wrong. At the same time, I felt the situation with dragging me off and the lack of communication wasn't addressed at all.'

We went on and played Antrim and the two boys, Colm and Tomás, came off the bench. It was a very unconvincing performance but coming down on the bus after the game in Tullamore, the draw was being made on the radio and as we all listened, it was announced: Kerry–Dublin, All-Ireland quarter-final.

We hit the ground running that day and never, ever looked back, winning by 17 points. Pat Gilroy made the infamous 'startled earwigs' comment in describing his team. I think we knew we were never going to be beaten after that.

We all started playing from the quarter-final, beating Meath in the last four and you had Tadhg Kennelly, who was absolutely lifting. It was amazing; he was injured with a broken bone in his hand and he was able to put these injuries to the back of his head, which I thought was phenomenal.

We beat Cork in the final. If it was a movie, when we won the All-Ireland against our near neighbours, after a drama-filled season, me and Jack would find each other in the middle of the pitch under the tickertape.

We'd both shrug, laugh and embrace. Never happened.

There was never any reconciliation or moment of mutual respect in the dressing room afterwards. There was never a shared moment of understanding reached in the snug of a bar over the subsequent days.

It was never that; it was all brushed under the carpet. Don't mention the war. At the end of the day, like anyone else, we three brothers were on the Kerry team because we were good enough.

But in my view, if there was any reason at all where it

was a tight call between one of us Ó Sés and another player, there's only one way that would have gone – against us. You really had to be as good as you were to be on the team.

It's a mirror image of the dynamic I experienced during my time playing under Páidí. Starting out as the manager's nephew, I felt I had to be *clearly* the better choice, because Páidí was harder on us. With Jack it was the same – but that came from a different place.

As well as that, it's often easier to handle things done to you, than things done to your family. I felt that Jack would have been harsh on Tomás – and I took it personally.

In the All-Ireland final in against Mayo in 2006, Jack substituted Tomás at half time. I think deep down, the reason went back a game against Longford in the qualifiers and Mossy Lyons was brought on for Tomás late on in the game.

Tomás went in, had his shower and just headed it off. But that would be Tomás. He just wasn't waiting around; he needed to get back to Cork. It wasn't a slight or a way of sending a message.

But I think Jack would have held a gripe. It was a power move, lacked class and betrayed what he thought of Tomás and us.

Jack, I'm sure, would say Tomás wasn't playing great. He wasn't. He was on Billy Joe Padden and maybe Billy Joe had caught a high ball or two or something like that. But with a player like Tomás, you must give them the opportunity to come out and right the wrongs. He had a lot of credit in the bank.

The same opportunity to right a wrong wasn't afforded to us on two occasions.

In 2009, against Sligo – infamously – and I suppose Tomás against Mayo, and Jack knew we were going to win those two games. Jack probably didn't think those games were going to go down to the wire; he would have envisaged they were gimmes.

I'm sure if that was a game now against Dublin or a Cork side or Tyrone, there's no way he would have whipped Tomás or me for that matter in those games, and I think he knew what he was at. And I thought that was a bit disrespectful again.

CHAPTER 22

MIND GAMES

In 2009, I missed the National League final against Derry in Croke Park after doing my medial ligament. We played Mayo in the league, beating them 13 points to 11 and I was playing centre back.

I played a lot of the league there and absolutely loved it out there, kicking ball through the lines, defending that patch. We won our first three games against Donegal, Tyrone and Derry.

In the second half of the fourth game against Mayo, Aidan O'Shea, who was carrying a bit of weight at the time, came down on top of me and I popped my knee. I thought the cruciate was done and that was game over for the season for me.

I went for the MRI to be told that it was the medial ligament, thanks be to God, and that I would be out for around 12 weeks.

Lying in the hospital bed, I opened the calendar app on my phone and worked out I'd be back in mid-June.

The first game was pencilled in against Cork for 7 June. I made it back in 10 weeks and the reason was the work of the coach, Alan O'Sullivan, who is still the coach with me with the school, The Green.

Alan would go into the then physio, Louise Smith, and say, 'Where are we with Marc now? What can we do tonight?' We'd go out onto the pitch from 6:30 p.m. until 7 p.m., and myself and Pádraig Reidy, who was injured too, would do our work with Alan. As well as that, everything I was asked to do in the gym and on the pitch, I was doing it.

I got back and played a club game against Kerins O'Rahillys and I was marking Barry John Walsh. It was my first time playing football in 10 weeks and I was inside in the full back line, twisting and turning. The knee was under serious pressure and if there was ever going to be a test this was it.

Barry John did well on me on the night, getting a couple of points, and I found the going tough, but I was back. I was rusty, but what Alan O'Sullivan did for me in those three months was never forgotten. I wouldn't have been where I was only for him.

When Jack came in first, he introduced a sports psychologist to the group.

Declan Coyle was a lovely man and was excellent at his

job. Jack was using Declan himself and evidently getting a lot out of it and wanted us to have the same benefit. But I was not interested in talking to him.

As a player and now as a coach, I completely understand the role of sports psychologists. I think they're a positive thing, but to get anything from sports psychology, it must come down to the individual.

It's like anything – if somebody is going to start training, lose a few pounds or give up cigarettes or drink, the person needs to want to do it.

For me that's what it's like with sports psychologists; the player has to say, 'I think that'd be good, yeah, that'd help.'

We used to listen to this guy talk about the two different platforms: broadly speaking, there's the positive platform and the negative platform, the glass half empty or the glass half full. (I'd deny I had any glass at all, if Jack asked, of course.)

It worked for certain fellas; there's no doubt about that.

Darragh wasn't into it and he made sure this man knew where he stood. I wasn't as bald-headed but I made sure to avoid any direct contact.

Then, after playing a National League game, Jack said, 'Marc, will you talk to Declan?'

And I said, 'No, I'm okay, but thanks.'

'You'll have to talk to him,' Jack said.

I said, 'No, I'm okay, Jack. Thanks.'

This went on for a bit but I played down the clock.

We played a game against Monaghan in the 2006 league, with me at centre back and it went fine. I scored a point and there was no drama. But Jack must have seen something in the game that made him think I wasn't right.

'You need to talk to a sports psychologist,' he said to me afterwards.

'No, Jack, I'm actually okay, but thanks again.'

'No, Marc, either you speak to the sports psychologist now or you'll be sitting down.'

'You know what, Jack,' I fired back, 'if you need to put me sitting down, put me sitting down. But I'm not talking to a sports psychologist. End of.'

That was the end of that then. But I didn't appreciate the pressure he was putting on me, thinking he was going to press-gang me into talking to this man. I just felt that was again disrespectful and it didn't sit easy with me.

I had nothing whatsoever against Declan. It just wasn't for me at that stage. And I know from dealing with players that he would benefit guys, but I knew my job and what I had to do and I didn't need another person to tell me what to do.

My reluctance had nothing to do with the fact Declan was 'Jack's man'. I'd totally bought into playing with Kerry. If I thought a conversation with him would bring us one step closer to the Sam Maguire, I would have jumped onto the leather chaise longue and spilled my guts.

I just thought that all I needed to get my head right was

to be training hard and knowing where my body needed to be and if my body was right, I knew I was going to be able to perform.

As the phrase goes, healthy body, healthy mind. It worked for me up to now. I also knew that when the ground hardened come April, that was my time.

With my game, I struggled slightly in certain league games when underfoot conditions were a bit softer. But then when the ground firmed up, I was able to get that extra yard. I was hopping off the ground and I knew that it didn't take much to get me right.

Of course, if I played poorly in training, I'd go home and I wouldn't sleep. All I wanted to do was get back into training the next night and to put it right. I might sound old school, but that was my sports psychology – fairly simple and straightforward, but if you look at it down the years, I don't think it did me any wrong. It's not as though I'm this kind of backward fellow who disagrees with all uses of sports psychology.

It's just it wasn't for me and I know there were a few more fellas who felt the same. Some were vocal about it; some didn't want to talk to him.

The Saturday night before one of our All-Ireland finals, Ger Keane, our physio, did a session of relaxation therapy with us.

He told us to bring a pillow down to one of the hotel

conference rooms and after we all lay down flat on the carpet floor.

We closed our eyes as he half-whispered instructions like, 'Relax every bone in your body,' and 'Feel the breathing,' and all this.

Of course, with a group of 30-odd young men someone would make a fart noise and the place would explode laughing or there'd be various quips that would get us chuckling again while Ger was trying to get us to be in the moment. It's fair to say not everyone bought into the value of this exercise. But Ger was an amazing, positive influence on the group and the players loved him.

Ger, in fairness, would get a bit of calm again and we'd get through the session.

We got up to go afterwards but Séamus Scanlon remained sprawled out. He was full-on asleep and snoring on the ground. We had to nudge him to wake him up – we have an All-Ireland final here, Séamus.

'Jesus, man,' he said, 'that was the most relaxed I've felt in a long time.'

Warm-weather camps were always an important part of our preparation too. We'd been away with Páidí but you'd be hard pushed to argue there was much physical benefit to what we engaged in.

Our first training trip was during Jack O'Connor's first spell in charge with Pat Flanagan overseeing training in La

Santa in Lanzarote. Honestly, it was one of the most physically intense experiences I've ever endured – and it was beneficial.

The itinerary was packed. We did three sessions per day, starting at 8 a.m. with an hour's running.

Then we had the breakfast and went back to bed for a bit. We were roused again at noon and played football from 1 p.m. for an hour or so. Into the pool next for some recovery, a bit of lunch, rest and the day was rounded out with an evening gym session.

That was repeated over the course of six days – it added up and you can imagine it was as advantageous as a month's worth of work at home. As a teacher, I'm not one to advocate cramming – but this was priceless to us. As well as the obvious physical benefit, the psychological effect was almost tangible.

We climbed the steps of the plane – gingerly after a tough week – knowing we'd a huge bank of work done. That gave us confidence in our fitness. We weren't going to be behind anyone when it came to strength and conditioning.

Of course, we returned home with plenty of new anecdotes and in jokes that make up the ties that bind any group. One story that was often referred to later in the year involved Séamus Scanlon.

The complex had a huge pool with a diving board, which must have been 50 feet high. We all launched ourselves into the water with Séamus, who couldn't swim, watching on. Despite this fact, he decided to have a go at the high diving board, after asking a group of us to wait for him when he hit the water and get him to safety.

If a team-building consultant wanted to concoct a trust exercise, they couldn't have come up with anything more dramatic than this.

Séamus bravely took the plunge but when he hit the water he started flailing violently. I was the first man on the scene and I got an elbow square in the nose and William Kirby eventually got Scanlon to the safety of the side of the pool.

On another camp, the manager gave us licence to blow off some steam. Big mistake.

It ended with one of our party taking a dig in the face and suffering a significant injury. That incident flashed the lights for our nights out. We were there to work.

One day much later during Éamonn Fitzmaurice's reign as Kerry manager, a lush patch of grass in the state-of-the-art Quinta de Lago resort was transformed into my parents' lawn … and Tomás and I were children again, as so often happened.

It was a beautiful morning in Portugal in the middle of a warm-weather camp.

We were instructed to run a simple drill. You'd get a ball, pass it to a fella, you'd receive it back, you'd hit the tackle bag, you'd pass it to another fella, you'd receive it back.

And just as you receive it … you're hitting the tackle bag again. What could possibly go wrong?

Earlier that morning, Tomás had done something to me. Like so many times in our childhood at Ard an Bhóthair, 'he started it'. He'd tripped me at the start of the session and I thought to myself, *I'm going to get him back.*

During the drill I got the ball and I had a bit of momentum coming and I said to myself, *I'm gonna fucking drill this fella into the ground.* But Tomás knows me well, and he saw me coming.

His Kerry training gear might as well have been a matador costume as he pulled the tackle bag away from me at the last moment and I went absolutely flying. It was a morning with a nice carpet of dew on the grass, which lubricated my momentum.

I'm not joking when I say I went for 10 yards – absolutely flying away from the rest of the session. The whole training session came to a halt and there were 30 lads keeled over laughing at me. The worst thing was seeing Tomás roaring laughing like a schoolboy, calling me an eejit.

I had to get up and dust myself down and take my medicine.

As well as knowing my own body and mind, I grew up watching, consciously or otherwise, what it took to play for Kerry. What it took to prepare properly. What it meant to live with the pressure. How to handle the highs and lows.

I was taking that in like the sea air and the music in Páidí's.

It wasn't until you won your All-Ireland that you could say that you were a Kerry footballer and I remember then after 2004 it was like the shackles were off.

Now I could express myself. That's the way I felt and my performances improved then afterwards. Páidí used to say a good player will win an All-Ireland, but a very good player will win two.

We've seen great players down through the years never win one – like Lee Keegan, who for me is probably the best player ever *not* to win an All-Ireland. People talk about Dermot Earley, Ciarán Whelan and Ciarán McDonald. They were great players, but Lee Keegan matched it with the very best of them and, alas, fell just short.

Winning one helped me build that confidence. The fact that I was there and then I think being given kind of the responsibility to mark big players and big games gave me great confidence. The fact these people trusted me to do a job was huge for me.

On the other side of it was Jack, who never played for Kerry. He became a very successful manager, but he never was in that situation as a player. I don't know if there were insecurities with him but we respected him as a very good coach.

Despite – or maybe because of – growing up in a well-known football family, I certainly had plenty of insecurities of my own. Was I good enough? Would I be in my brothers' shadow forever? They were there up as far as 2004.

CHAPTER 23

A TEAM OF BACHELORS

When Éamonn Fitzmaurice came in, he did a lot of work on building the culture, breaking down cliques and getting us all rowing the same way.

One year he brought us over to the English rugby club Harlequins who were under the leadership of former Ireland full back, Conor O'Shea.

Éamonn was big on the All Blacks and adopted their so-called no dickheads rule too. Early in 2014, he took us on a weekend away – if anyone thought they might get a few pints in after an afternoon white board session, they were disappointed.

We were given a list of things that we had to bring with us – a swimming cap, boots, outrageous stuff like your club socks, a tin of Batchelors baked beans, a pair of runners.

What is going on there?

We were told to meet in Killarney at 6 o'clock on Saturday morning. Some optimists thought, *This is great, we must be going somewhere exotic.*

But no, the bus made its way through some forest around the Galtees and we were ordered to get out and start jogging. This was to be an ultimate hell session and, as the name implies, wasn't going to be an enjoyable day out.

We hadn't a clue where we were exactly or what was in store as we jogged along with our bags of beans strapped to our backs for about three kilometres.

I'm looking at a few fellas who are struggling, and though it's awful to see, when you're in difficulty and you're going through pain, it's funny to see someone suffering worse than you.

Sometimes too, things are so bad, they're funny. We got to a clearing in the forest and the well-known army guy, Ray Goggins, and his team were there and there was all sorts of shouting and roaring at us. All the medals you might have had are no good to you at this stage.

It was tense and we were all shooting glances at each other and thinking, *What the fuck has Éamonn got us into here.*

We were told to get out our club colours from our bags and put on gas masks. Daithí Casey from Dr Crokes, who was a young lad at the time, gave a little nervous giggle out of him. That singled him out anyway for more abuse.

Then these army rangers who Goggins was leading, told us to get out our tins of Batchelors beans. I knew I was in trouble because I had packed a tin of Heinz beans, which would be my preference.

I surreptitiously slipped the wrapper off and then, using all my cunning, disingenuously said, 'Hey, what smart fucker is after taking the wrapper off my tin of beans?'

I was awarded 50 press-ups on the soft forest floor for my troubles. That was then doubled to 100 because I had no goggles either, it transpired. Meanwhile, Casey – in a gas mask – was jogging on the spot next to me for five minutes. That was the getting-to-know-you period. After that we broke into little teams.

You know in *Armageddon* when Owen Wilson asks what it's going to be like on the asteroid if the mission succeeds in landing the crew?

'Two hundred degrees in the sunlight, minus 200 in the shade, canyons of razor-sharp rock, unpredictable gravitational conditions, unexpected eruptions, things like that.'

'Okay,' Wilson sums up, 'so the scariest environment imaginable. Thanks. That's all you gotta say, scariest environment imaginable.'

That was going through my mind – because it was the complete unknown. *What the fuck is going to happen here?*

When we got into our teams, we had to see about building things while the army boys continued – with great glee, I thought – breaking us down. They were telling us how shit we were and how fucking useless we were at this and that.

After a while of more of the reckless exercises where we were running around the place in gas masks and going from press-ups to sit-ups, they eventually pulled us out and started interrogating us about our actions.

'What should you have done in this situation?'

'I should have told my team to do this or that,' we were mumbling. But whatever we said it was wrong.

'Oh, you're a big man, are you?' or 'You're a bit of a fucking maverick,' and they'd try to ridicule you in front of the group. You basically had to take your medicine.

'No, sir, I was wrong there. I shouldn't have done that.' You wouldn't want to have any self-esteem issues anyway.

That was the warm-up for the mountain: Galtee Mor. We had to jog up and everyone had to carry something. Fellas had medicine balls, gear bags, food. But at least we were getting away from the lunatics below.

We got a few breaks and – if you know Galtee Mor – you'll know where's a bit of a false summit. It's like that bit in *The Simpsons* where Homer looks up at the Murderhorn and gulps.

'No that's it over there, Homer.'

It nearly broke my heart. But we got to the top and it was Baltic up there; there was a strong wind blowing up the side of the mountain and no one wanted to hang around, despite the lovely view. Fitzmaurice called on two of the bags that had been hauled up the side of the mountain. They contained two sets of Kerry jerseys.

He gave us all a jersey each – so there were two players in each position, as such. Éamonn gave me a No 2 shirt and he gave Shane Enright the same. The message was implicit: you're fighting with each other for that shirt for the year.

He said a few words and he let us know there was no one guaranteed their jersey. We all heard him loud and clear. Before he finished, he said, 'This is going to be our year. We're going to surprise everyone. We're going to do whatever it takes.'

It was a moment that helped with team spirit and team bonding because later in the season, when we were out training, you'd be saying to yourself, *This is tough* – but the memory of that day would help you get through it. Nothing can be as difficult as that.

Getting back down was the next challenge. We ran down and picked up a bit of speed. As the herd was trundling down, Declan O'Sullivan suddenly fell into a massive hole. How one of our star forwards managed to come out of it without a broken leg, I will never know.

In a team-building exercise that wasn't on Ray Goggins' itinerary, we had to pull Declan out of the hole. His runner was still stuck inside, so he reached down into the darkness pulled out the sneaker which was destroyed and he just flung it down the mountain with a roar. He ran off after it and down the mountain, destroyed in muck, wearing a single shoe.

We all followed him down in tears laughing.

There wasn't a word spoken on the bus back home. Not a peep out of anyone. We got dropped to our cars and crawled into them as broken men. It took me a full week to recover from that – I was spent, genuinely. Mentally and physically, I was in bits for seven days afterwards.

But, though we were shells for some time afterwards, it helped us with our preparation for the year. We were a unit. My body ultimately felt stronger afterwards, which helped me mentally.

We played Mayo in the All-Ireland semi-final in what turned out to be an epic two-game series.

All year long there were probably seven defenders going for six positions.

In the first game Killian Young was dropped and Peter Crowley was back in. Fionn Fitzgerald was struggling with Andy Moran and I was moved on to him. I knew it would be a tough assignment.

I marked Andy in the 2011 All-Ireland semi-final and there were 100 yards of space in front of the two of us. It was like trying to keep the tide out. I kept him to two points but it was a highly stressful afternoon's work.

He was the type of player who'd make five or six runs and wouldn't get the ball. Meanwhile you're exhausted from chasing after him – and the next run would be rewarded with a pass in.

He was the most honest inside forward I've marked. Some forwards would just be static but would know when to make the run, but Moran would be over and back, over and back and then he'd get the ball and he'd go straight at you.

The best of forwards go straight at you. Michael Meehan and Alan Brogan did it, Con O'Callaghan does it now and it's so hard to stop that type of player.

We were struggling against Mayo and being beaten in the middle of the field. Éamonn rolled the dice and Donaghy entered the fray well into the 60s. It was go for broke. The ball came out to David Moran on the right inside, a diagonal ball across to Donaghy, who won it. He gave a lovely quick pass to James O'Donoghue and it was in the back of the net.

For the equaliser, I tore down the field and the ball was about to go over the end line into the Davin End and I just about managed to win it, press the brakes, turn and swing a pass. The ball was out to Kieran O'Leary and over the bar. It was a draw.

Barry John Keane caught the kick out and Bryan Sheehan had a huge opportunity to kick a winner well outside the 45. It didn't go over and we went again.

So it went to a replay – a replay in Limerick because of an American football game in Croke Park.

*

The first day in Croke Park, there was a member of the Mayo backroom team who was constantly in and out and he was particularly verbal – and opinionated – about me.

He'd come in and he'd say, 'Come on Andy. His legs are fucked. He's useless. He's fucking useless.'

And if I could, I would have caught a hold of him before he was gone again. I was totally bemused but became more and more preoccupied with catching this fella. His intention was obviously to take my focus and for a few minutes it certainly worked.

Of course, I never did, but when the whistle went and we'd drawn, he was at the front of my thoughts for the replay.

I was back in Jimmy O'Shea's Texaco in Blennerville midweek, to get a bag of coal, and I got a phone call from Éamonn Fitzmaurice on the Tuesday.

'Come here, Marc,' he says. 'We're not going with you for the replay.'

It's like one of those moments when you know where you were at that exact time and what you were doing. It was like a bolt of lightning. I just could not believe it.

All the while, when all these kind of seven-into-six debates were happening, I never thought for one second that I was going to be dropped.

I didn't think I deserved to lose out. I wasn't playing to the best of my ability, but I think Éamonn was probably judging me on my own standards. I thought I had enough credit in the bank and, despite that, I was playing better than some of the other fellas.

'Look Éamonn,' I said on the phone, 'I think you're making the wrong call here. I respect your decision but I think you're wrong.'

He was the manager. He was doing his job. It's fair to say I was seriously pissed off though, naturally.

But I fully got that Éamonn was making the decision he thought was correct for the team and I wasn't going to be throwing the toys out of the pram. Quite the opposite.

In the team meeting before the game, I stood up and said, 'Lads, there's a prick going around with water and he's acting the bollix with the verbals. If you get the chance, get a hold of him.'

I might have been less than happy to be unceremoniously dropped for what was a great occasion and a huge game – but I was still going to contribute. Marking everyone's card for this fella, was a start.

'Make sure you take no shit out there from anyone coming onto the pitch,' I said to underline the point. Often, a message in a meeting is most powerful when someone who doesn't usually speak up has something to say.

And Anthony Maher, the quietest player on the team, jumped up, obviously exercised by the point I made. 'Yeah, yeah, that fucking guy!' he said 'Jesus Christ. He's a right prick. He's coming on throwing himself about. I swear to God, lads, if he comes on the field the next day, I'm gonna grab him by the ears and pull him off the fucking pitch.'

It set the tone very nicely. I was pissed off not to be playing but delighted to be contributing and seeing Maher get so animated.

As well as the water carrier, I had a bee in my bonnet about Kevin McLaughlin. He was a player anyone would love to have on their team any day of the week – maybe a lot like Paul Galvin.

But Kevin could take a lot of credit for the new Football Review Committee rules being introduced because if you went to take a free, he'd stand in front you, while being cute about it.

He wouldn't do it blatantly. He'd let on that he was turning around here actually to kind of go back. But all the while he was in the way. And if you tried to move to the right, he'd go that way, but pretend he wasn't looking.

He was a master at it and adept at throwing the ball away, especially if the ref was distracted. So, I was saying to myself, *If I get on, I'm going to have a go at that fella.*

But I really didn't think I'd get on. When a match is in the melting point, a corner back is never the lad you send on from the bench. Unless someone is having a nightmare altogether, it's rare a back is going to get in, especially in the first half. But unfortunately for Shane Enright he dragged down Cillian O'Connor for a penalty and Andy Moran was causing wreck.

Shane probably should have got a red card but escaped with a booking. Éamonn gave me the nod on the bench and I was on after 20 minutes or so.

It was a Saturday evening; the Gaelic Grounds was creaking at the seams with partisan Kerry and Mayo supporters. With a place in the championship decider on the line, it was set up for a classic. I tore onto the pitch, a man on a mission, with the score 7 points to 1.

The first ball I got, I raced up the line, on the right inside the terrace side. I just wanted to go that way and bring the game up the field.

I was on my old college friend Alan Dillon and I knew I'd have the legs on him and I resolved to put him going the other way because I knew he'd find it uncomfortable. He was taken off, and slowly but surely, we started to turn the screw.

Donaghy got a goal. We ground our way back into it. And then I think a hugely significant part in that game was the clash of heads between Cillian O'Connor and Aidan O'Shea. Two of Mayo's most dangerous men clashed heads in the first half and both left the field with blood injuries and after being assessed at half time, did not re-enter the fray until into the second half.

I think that had a huge bearing on the game.

There are key moments in games where you have the luck or you don't have the luck.

I think if you look at the 2016 All-Ireland semi-final, Peter Crowley being checked by Kevin McMenamin, that would have been a point for Kerry, but then Diarmuid Connolly went down the other end of the field and he kicked an incredible point. I'm not saying we would have beaten Dublin but it could have been a drawn game. Instead, it was a two-point game. We had no luck.

But we had the luck that day against Mayo.

I got up the field in the second half and I kicked a score and I knew that even going into extra time, I had it in the legs. A melee broke out and I caught a hold of Kevin McLaughlin and I just grabbed him to the ground and Donaghy is trying to restrain me or pull me away from him.

In the background, you can see Anthony Maher pulling the famous water carrier off the field with his bare hands. We were ready for the battle and it was a tight game and that was a great Mayo team. But we managed to get over the line.

When the whistle went, the emotion came out of me. I was going through a tough time anyway off the pitch and then I'd been dropped – to end the week on the pitch, having done my bit for my teammates in an absolute cauldron – it was hugely satisfying.

And I expressed that emotion by doing an out-of-character

jig on the spot. I'm not sure where it came from. My team-mates were quick to jump on this public expression of joy and Tomás informed me I looked like a fool, of course, as only older brothers can.

The following week when we were in a tactical session, the video guys had clipped it up and slowed down the footage. It was funny and just a release of emotions.

I was delighted I'd proven the management wrong too. There was a lot going on and football was my only outlet. The Ó Sés aren't ones for therapy. So, when that outlet is taken from you, it's challenging.

After the game, another battle fought and won together, myself and Éamonn embraced.

'I know Marc well,' he'd just told the media, 'and I knew when I took the job that it would be difficult if I had to leave out players that I played with.

'I know the stock that Marc comes from and I knew there would be a severe reaction when he came on the pitch and I think that was visible for everyone to see.'

I caught him and pointed, saying, 'I told you; you were wrong.'

'You'll be playing for the final,' he said, as we were cheered up the tunnel.

Earlier in the year, Éamonn got us to write out our personal priorities for the season. The night before the Munster final with Cork, he reminded us all of the goals down in Fota.

I would have kept it simple – win the National League, win the Munster championship and win the All-Ireland. I wouldn't have said winning All Stars or anything like that. Reading about Michael Darragh MacAuley, he told his father that he was going to win Footballer of the Year. That wouldn't have been my answer at that late stage of my career.

Éamonn was good at finding the right tone when addressing a group – and his timing was important. In 2004, we probably went onto the pitch emotionally exhausted after a great, emotive speech before the All-Ireland club final with An Ghaeltacht.

The timing of Fitzmaurice's meetings were very good, and they were measured in that they were very calm. He just went through what we had to do.

He referenced different teams too and had a particular *grá* for the All Blacks – the no dickheads thing, cleaning the dressing rooms, all that – and he called in various favours I'm sure to get interesting speakers into the camp.

Ronan O'Gara landed in one day and Roy Keane was lined up but, as a Cork man, he thought better of it. The night before the 2014 All-Ireland, Ray Goggins walked in and I was transported back to the Galtee Mor. What a nightmare.

CHAPTER 24

SERVE THE BEST WINE LAST

We had our homework done on Donegal for the final. Two years previously Jim McGuinness had masterminded a good win over us in the quarter-final.

We naively left ourselves totally open and we were punished. Colm McFadden kicked three or four points off me. I was tearing down the field and then Donegal were catching us on the counter.

Michael Murphy and McFadden destroyed us and we didn't play as a defensive team at all. So not long after the Limerick drama, Éamonn got a hold of me and told me I'd be on McFadden.

I had a job to do and I completely tuned in. I owed him one.

*

The night before the final, there was a letter to each player from Éamonn slipped under our hotel room doors. I wouldn't be one for sentimentality so I don't have the letter, but the message stayed with me.

Éamonn wrote that I had faced the storm head on throughout the season and come through the other end. There were also references to McFadden's threat and that I would do the job and keep him scoreless in our duel.

Earlier that night, we had our team meeting and I sat back watching the younger players in the room, trying to gauge how they were feeling, when Aidan O'Mahony spoke up.

'Look lads,' he said, 'I'm marking Michael Murphy tomorrow. I'm telling you, I'm going to do my job. I am going to beat Michael Murphy tomorrow. I am. I'm not going to let the side down. I will make sure that I do everything in my power to do my job. If everyone else inside in the room here promises to do their job, we will win the game.'

Talk can be cheap but in all my years involved in the team I've never been so convinced by something I heard in a meeting room. I was buying everything he was selling and I could tell everyone else was convinced too.

In my first All-Ireland I'd pulled a pair of boxers out of my gear bag that were way too big for me. In 2014, my boots gave me some discomfort.

I always just loved the Adidas Predator Manias and I had a few pairs of them. I strapped them on for the final against Donegal and they were kind of multi-studs. I found you have more comfort in them and that's why I wore them generally.

In the first few minutes I remember slipping two or three times and I was absolutely petrified that I would lose my footing. As a keen student of the game, my mind went back to the 1995 All-Ireland semi-final – Cork's Mark O'Connor against Dublin's Jason Sherlock. Jayo slipped him and the Rebels' full back went flying and Jayo put the ball in the back of the net. I always felt that the last line of defence, it's a kamikaze decision to wear a pair of multi-studs. And here I was, trying to stay upright and get through the half.

I couldn't wait to get to halftime to change my boots to the proper Preds with steel studs, especially as Croke Park is a slippy pitch anyway. I got in and sorted it and thankfully got out in the second half feeling more confident.

Aidan promised to do his job, and he delivered with an awesome performance. While Murphy did have a big effect on the game, he didn't have the oversized influence of a legend of the sport, as he usually would.

Kieran Donaghy was upset after not getting a minute in the quarter-final. In the days afterwards Éamonn put his hands up at training and conceded to Kieran that he should have been brought on.

In the final, he was the man of the match, bagging 1–2 in a game we won with a very un-Kerry scoreline: 2–9 to Donegal's 0–12. We had the luck too with the goals.

Paul Geaney struck early on, finishing beautifully, after he gathered after a mishit from Stephen O'Brien. And Donaghy pounced on Durkin's kick out to punish him. His goal was so important for us.

I knew from years of training with him never to bring a ball out if I saw Donaghy. I'd avoid bringing the ball into contact with him at all costs.

Cillian O'Connor of Mayo was similar and our own Johnny Crowley back in the day; they were incredible tacklers, getting their arms around you and ripping the ball away like an NFL defensive lineman.

Donaghy was brilliant at putting goalkeepers off by placing his huge figure in front of them. You can go back to his goal against Cork in 2007 where he takes the ball off Ger Spillane too, coming out of the defence.

Towards the end of the game, I was marking McFadden and Donegal were coming. They were converging on goal and I felt I had to kind of go back in towards the goal. Next thing, the ball ricochets out to McFadden, who's in the corner, and he hits the post.

If that had gone in, it would have been a draw and then they'd have the momentum, but thankfully it popped back out.

*

It was Kerry's 37th All-Ireland but the first as underdogs since Páidí's team was inspired by Bomber Liston in 1978 and shocked the Dubs. It was also my fifth Celtic Cross and the sweetest of them all.

The first one was so important and franked my credentials as a Kerry player. But this one meant a lot too – coming back into the team, turning my season around in that memorable semi-final in Limerick and ending with this special final.

I have a lovely photograph of myself and my nephew, Níall, where I'm lifting him up, I have Sam in the other arm and Ellen is in the background. It's lovely and great memories. It was nice to be given the space to take it in.

I know they say that, in Páidí's day, when the supporters were left onto the pitch at full time in an All-Ireland it was incredible. But to me it was kind of chaotic too.

We had days when we lost and the other side's fans were on the field and it could be scary. There were some of our fellas getting belts from Tyrone supporters coming off the pitch after the heartbreak of an All-Ireland final defeat.

After all this toil, Maurice Fitzgerald never got to go up the Hogan Stand steps in 1997, because he was just mauled by Kerry supporters and he always said he had to get back again to go up the steps. I can see both sides. It's enjoyable for the winners' supporters when they get onto the field.

It's something myself and Dara Ó Cinnéide completely disagree on. He feels that it's the players and the fans that own Croke Park and the supporters should be allowed on the pitch after finals.

But I always think of it as a health and safety issue and it's just chaotic. And when the players can celebrate, then they're able to celebrate in front of the supporters. They can go around the pitch, like we did that day.

Like the supporters, my brothers too were in the stands. It was my first All-Ireland without them next to me and the first that Páidí wasn't around to witness.

I thought about him a lot that Sunday. He'd be the first man to ring you and arrange to meet for a pint and a debrief afterwards and he really would have enjoyed that All-Ireland.

My brothers too, of course, were quick to congratulate me – even if, for Tomás, it meant I'd equalled his haul of five medals. It's no harm, I couldn't have finished up with him having that over me.

He was now part of the RTÉ coverage and asked during the year what made Kerry so good at the accurate foot-passing that was seen as the key to unlocking blanket defences. He deadpanned: 'It's called football, Des.'

Darragh still led the way amongst us with six but he wouldn't needle you like Tomás. Regardless, you still know where you are in the pecking order in Kerry.

Earlier in the year, the two boys were on a fundraising

trip to New York with the likes of Mikey Sheehy and Ógie Moran – two lads, like Páidí, who then had the record eight All-Irelands.

One morning Bomber Liston approached Darragh and said, 'Hey, Minus Two, come over to our table.' It was early in the morning for this craic and Darragh was bemused. 'What's that, Eoin?' he said.

'Yeah,' says Bomber, 'You're Minus Two because you only have the half dozen medals. Don't worry, they're calling me Minus One.'

It goes without saying, I was happy to be on five – or minus three on the Kerry scorecard. It was an amazing feeling that was completely different to all the other ones that came before. Did I think it was going to be the last one? I didn't. But whatever about the medals, and they were great, it's the memories I appreciate, and that moment will live long.

After the game, in the players' lounge I saw Rory Kavanagh, an old friend from Maynooth.

I had faced Alan Dillon in the semi-final, another great friend of ours from college.

Back then we were a handy soccer team. We played in a big football competition – five or six of us – during RAG week one year in college. There was €300 in the pot for the winners so that focused our minds.

The whole college were in the tournament seemingly

and our team was made up of Dillon, Kavanagh – who was a lovely soccer player – and a few other handy lads.

We managed to win the cup and the money and – you guessed it – went on the piss for two days. It probably cost us money in the end. Then years later we're coming up against each other in the final.

In the players' lounge afterwards, I immediately saw Rory and his wife Kathryn who was at college with us as well and who I know well too. That players' lounge is a strange place in the hour after an All-Ireland. On one side, there are players celebrating and the other side there are players who are just totally demoralised.

I've been on both sides of the room.

That night Ellen travelled home as Alice was starting school the following day, so my dinner date turned out to be Gooch and Declan. I sat down with them at the reception and felt completely at ease. Those are the evenings when the pundits reflect on the final and the season and pick teams of the year on *The Sunday Game*. In previous years, as a younger player, I may have been keen to get the recognition for my year's work and represent Kerry on those selections.

And I was so lucky to get individual awards down through the years. In 2014, however, I was just happy we pulled off this unlikely win. I wasn't even listening. I was just happy to have my All-Ireland medal, drink my pint of Guinness and speak to my teammates.

*

The best pints of all are the day after an All-Ireland victory when you're coming down on the train. It's just a craic and the banter, after making the stop into Hughie, a great friend of Páidí's, in the Boar's Head on Capel Street that morning.

Shane Lowry was inside there the same morning and congratulated us before we hopped on the bus to Heuston. We stopped off in Rathmore because the minor team had won the All-Ireland as well and Shane Ryan was in goal for them and we had Aidan and Paul Murphy with the senior team.

It's always the first stop and then it's on to Tralee and later Killarney. First-world problems, but it can become a long journey, hopping on and off and climbing onto stages. I'd sometimes slip away and meet a couple of friends in a quiet bar. That would suit me better. I did that in Killarney that night as I was tired at that stage anyway. Then you're into Tuesday – a day when a lot of the responsibilities have been discharged and the players can relax together. Then, back to work on Wednesday.

The headmaster in the local school in the Gaeltacht made the point to me that over the previous few years no player had brought the Sam Maguire Cup to the primary schools.

I explained I'd taken so many days off school at that stage to facilitate the actual winning of the cup that I didn't have much wiggle room. But I told him that if he'd write a note to the principal of my school and she was okay with me going back west with the cup, I'd go back to the schools and do all the primary schools.

I got the nod and I was able to bring Sam around to all the primary schools in the Gaeltacht, where my nephews and nieces were and all our neighbours' kids. That was so enjoyable for me but an important thing to do too to show them what the tradition means.

One of my earliest memories – maybe my first – was Páidí bringing the Sam Maguire to Ard an Bhóthair in 1985 as captain. I've never forgotten it. It was nice to close the circle.

I took plenty of questions from the kids. 'Did you always want to play for Kerry?' 'Messi or Ronaldo?' 'What was your favourite win?'

As well as my own comeback story and the fact no one gave us a chance after Gooch's injury or the roasting to Cork, the answer to the latter was easy. The 2014 All-Ireland is without doubt my favourite one.

CHAPTER 25

GREEN FINGERS AND BLACK CARDS

After a high can come the fall. In 2015, I tripped coming down the stairs and broke my coccyx. Sore thing. It meant I was sidelined for much of the league campaign.

At the time, Éamonn was trying to evolve the team a bit, which is always wise. We had players like Paul Murphy, Fionn Fitzgerald, Pa Kilkenny and Mark Griffin who were making their mark. Mark Griffin, Jonathan Lyne, Jack Sherwood all started against Dublin in the National League in Killarney and Kerry had a good win: 15 points to 1–10.

There were players like that getting their game and there was a new look to the side. I was watching on for Game 4 of the league, when Cork absolutely hammered us 3–17 to 2–9.

It wasn't until game 6 that I came back in after that coccyx injury, but I wouldn't say I ever fully recovered. Even to this day if I'm sitting down having a cup of tea or if I stay in the same position for long enough it gets sore.

In the championship, we beat Tipperary well in Semple Stadium, 2–14 to 2–8, and we had more of the 2014 team back in, in terms of the backs at least, except for Aidan O'Mahony who was coming back from injury as well.

We played Cork in Killarney and were very lucky to get a replay. With the game on the line in the last moments, Fionn Fitzgerald got the ball and was trying to put it into the square with the last kick of the game. It went straight over the bar. Pure pox, although Fionn still argues he was going for a point.

Páirc Uí Chaoimh was being redeveloped at the time so Cork would have to come back to Killarney. The story went that every publican in Killarney was happy to stand Fionn a free pint.

The following week was played in an absolute deluge. It just did not stop raining for the entire match. It's a lesson for younger players, playing in conditions like that – the main thing that you had to do was make sure you were staying on your feet. You do not allow your forward inside you because it could be a goal all day long. Cork ended up ruing the missed opportunity the first day; we won 1–11 to 1–6. It wasn't one for the purists.

*

That wasn't that long ago but the championship has transformed since then. That was on 18 July and we weren't out again until 8 August against Kildare, so we were 'allowed' go out on the town for a pint.

Normally that walk from Fitzgerald Stadium down to the centre of Killarney, having beaten Cork in a Munster final, is one of the nice parts of a championship. But we put on the so-called going-out clothes heading down and were absolutely soaked to the skin by the time we got to the Towers in Killarney, where we were having food.

Having our bit to eat together, we felt we were in a good position to defend our All-Ireland. We had recovered well from the week before and got our matchups right. And the bonus was that Paul Galvin was back. He had taken a year out, having put his body on the line for Kerry for years previously and it needed a break.

Can you imagine all the belts he took out there in the middle of the field, especially given that Paul's game was based on breaking ball, putting himself in harm's way. He'd suffered from that point of view but he came back into the panel and it was a huge boost.

It probably put Éamonn under pressure straight away, given he and Paul are brothers-in-law. I knew myself, being an Ó Sé, what that was like. I realised Paul would have to go above and beyond to justify his existence, just to keep any grumbling to a whisper inside and outside the camp.

Naturally, you'd wonder if the players who were there in

Shaking hands with Kerry manager Éamonn Fitzmaurice after the Munster final in 2013 at Fitzgerald Stadium in Killarney. (© INPHO / Lorraine O'Sullivan)

I had enough on my plate trying to contain Bernard Brogan, let alone trying to take on three Dublin players! Thankfully, I managed to get my foot to the ball on this occasion. (© Brendan Moran / SPORTSFILE)

Coming off the pitch with my old sparring partner but good buddy Bernard Brogan. Dublin won that day in the 2013 All-Ireland semi-final, with Bernard getting the better of me on that occasion. (© INPHO / Donall Farmer)

Winning Sam for the last time in 2014, holding my nephew Niall at the same time, and with Ellen there in the background. One of the sweetest victories of them all! (© Brendan Moran / SPORTSFILE)

Tyrone used to bring out the best in me for some reason. Here I am getting down low to block a shot from Connor McAliskey in the All-Ireland semi-final in 2015. (© Dáire Brennan / SPORTSFILE)

Maurice Deegan giving me my marching orders on the same occasion. A black card meant you played no further part in the game. I didn't know it at the time but that day would be my last start in a Kerry jersey in championship. (© Brendan Moran / SPORTSFILE)

My last outing in Croke Park in 2016, coming off the pitch with Alice and our newborn, Tadhg. We had just lost to Dublin in the All-Ireland semi-final. I knew that was my last game, even though I hadn't announced my retirement yet. (© Dáire Brennan / SPORTSFILE)

Winning the county championship with An Ghaeltacht, here are the four of us celebrating at the Man of the Match function the day after. (© Eamonn Keogh / MacMonagle)

When I retired from Kerry, the Gaeltacht came calling. I became player/joint-manager with Conall Ó Cruadhlaoich. Here I am with a young Tadhg after winning my second intermediate medal, twenty years after winning my first. (© Don MacMonagle)

All-Ireland medals, 2004. The three of us in Killarney at the Gleneagle Hotel, receiving our All-Ireland medals. A proud moment for the family. (© Eamonn Keogh / MacMonagle)

On top of Mount Brandon at the launch of a traditional Irish music festival, here I am beside Jimmy Deenihan and leading musicians Emma Begley, Cuan Granville, Colin Sheehy, Cian Williams, Deirdre Granville, Ailbhe Johnson, Aoife Granville and Colm Bambury. (© Don MacMonagle)

The unveiling of my uncle's statue, with Páidí's former teammates Jimmy Deenihan, Denis Ógie Moran, Eoin Bomber Liston and, of course, the one and only Mick O'Dwyer, who sadly passed away earlier this year. (© Don MacMonagle)

All-Ireland final day, 2022, with my father-in-law, Tadhg, my son, Tadhg, and Alice. Huge excitement beforehand.

Back in Croke Park with Sam three years later, a cherished memory with Ellen and the kids after a great Kerry win over Donegal. (© James Keane)

With Ellen after our amazing wedding in Altea in Spain. Just married, the best feeling! (© Rafa Cortes Photographer)

With the three brothers at Marqués de Montemolar, Altea just after the wedding. (© Rafa Cortes Photographer)

Enjoying the wedding reception, taking a moment for a family picture with Ellen, Alice, Tadhg and Tom. Rounding off a perfect day. (© Rafa Cortes Photographer)

2014 and won Kerry an All-Ireland would be put out now that Paul was parachuted back in. I never heard it from them. Mikey Geaney and Jonathan Lyne had done well in 2014 and now suddenly Paul was back in and vying for that position with them. But I had no bother with it.

From the minute I heard Paul was coming back I was absolutely delighted because I knew what he could bring – even if it was just for 20 minutes per game at that stage of his life.

I loved playing with him throughout my career – what a personality and player – and he got better as the years went by. People talk about my brother Darragh back in the day, in the early 1990s, and how he supposedly wasn't a great kick passer at the start; but he ended up being the best kick passer in the country.

The same could be said for Galvin. His ability to kick the ball was just incredible. He'd pass the ball, be gone again, take it. And in no less a fillip to us, we had the best forward in the country returning too as Gooch was back from injury as well.

In those games against Cork, and the replay in particular, you'd Mikey Geaney coming off the bench; Peter Crowley, coming off the bench; Steven O'Brien, Paul Galvin, Barry John Keane and Gooch coming off the bench.

What do the South Africans call their subs? 'The Bomb Squad'. Any team in the country would kill for players of that calibre to come off the bench. And that was to supplement a starting team with the likes of Johnny Buckley, wing forward Bryan Sheehan, Donnchadh Walsh, Paul Geaney, Kieran Donaghy, James O'Donoghue. We had Maher and David Moran in the middle of the field, making it possibly 13 of the 15 starters nailed down. Éamonn had developed a very fixed team, a solid unit.

We were building nicely and things were looking good for me personally, until I decided to do a bit of gardening.

In the days before the Kildare game, I ordered a tonne of wood chips for the garden and I was planning on putting them down on the rockery in the back garden. Two days before the game I was tipping around doing the bit of work out the back. I had a wheelbarrow going with the chips up and down the garden and was content in my work.

After a while there was enough of the chips taken out of the bag that I reckoned I could pull the rest of them up. This was a couple of days before the game and I was 35 years of age at this stage. You'd have thought I'd have some sense by then.

I woke up the next day sore after all my squatting, twisting and pulling. I creaked as I climbed out of bed.

We were cruising in the game but I felt completely dead. I had no energy whatsoever. I put the hand up in the dressing room at half time and said, 'Look, the body isn't great. My legs just feel weak and I'm not feeling myself.'

I don't know if Éamonn thought that my body was getting

old but I didn't tell him I was pulling a tonne-bag of wood chips around the garden 24 hours previously. I stretched out on the bench and watched the lads finish the job at a canter: 7–16 to 10 points.

In the run up to the All-Ireland semi-final with Tyrone, I was flying. I was playing full back a lot of nights in training marking whoever – Donaghy, James, anyone who was coming into me – and things were going well.

Three or four days before the game, I jumped out of bed and cracked my big toe off the corner of the bed. Another sore one. I went down for an X-ray which showed that there was a fracture. Dr Mike Finnerty put an injection into it, strapped it up well, and I was good to go for the game.

I was full back on a wet day in Croke Park and it was one of those afternoons where I felt everything was going right for me. Whether it's experience, or achieving a flow state, being in the zone or just being lucky, I seemed to be in the right place at the right time; I was making the right decisions – the ball was hopping for me.

For 14 minutes at least.

In that first few minutes a ball then came out into the Hogan Stand side. I got up to it, managed to field it up in the air, kick pass and was gone up the field again looking for it. Moments later, Tyrone were through for a goal but I got in, got down on it and executed a good block.

I was stopping a few fires that day and felt things were

going well. I know over the years; Kerry have had a poor record on the biggest days against Tyrone. But whatever it was about them, they always brought out the best in me.

If nothing else, I was always up for it when I saw the Red Hand. But in the 14th or 15th minute of the game, I went down the Hogan Stand side, I was turned and before I knew it, I was rugby tackling my man to the ground.

Maurice Deegan, the ref, wasn't having it – I could see that as he approached. I could see the black card emerge and my day was over – this was the time you were gone and you could bring on a substitute.

It's tough going in those situations. I just had to sit there and stew. Ellen had brought then five-year-old Alice up to the game for the first time and it was probably her first time seeing me playing properly. And that was going through my mind as I slumped back in the seat.

Kerry pulled off a brilliant win without me, 0–18 to 0–11, with Barry John Keane, a grandson of 1955 Kerry captain John Dowling, kicking a super score. Though a lot of that team watched rather than lived through those three defeats against Tyrone in the noughties, it was a victory that healed some scarring.

It was the first time Kerry had beaten Tyrone in Croke Park since Páidí's vintage in 1986. That's not nothing. Little did I know that was the last time I'd start a championship game for Kerry.

*

It would have been a tougher day out if we'd lost, of course. But the lads got the job done against Tyrone and we had to prepare for another All-Ireland final – this time against the Dubs, who got past Mayo a week later.

I gave the toe a bit of a break and sat out the following week's work. My first session back I was marking Tom O'Sullivan, the new young Tom O'Sullivan, and he absolutely rinsed me. It was a brutal session for me; I'd say he kicked three or four points off me in training.

I just took to ground. Anytime I played poorly in a training session, I wouldn't sleep that night. I'd have to go home and give myself a talking to and come back to right the wrongs. And that would normally work out.

But I came back the next night to try and correct the record and unfortunately didn't play great again. That was now two sessions in a row that I wasn't myself. I couldn't put it down to anything other than that I had missed maybe 10 days of preparation. But those poor sessions accumulate like compound interest. I needed to get on top of it.

On the Saturday – 13 days out from the final – I tore my hamstring. I got an MRI and they found that it was a Grade 2 tear. Typically enough, I felt I could get back and I went to Éamonn and got my point across: 'Listen, I'll pass a fitness test. I'll get back.'

But no, Éamonn picked his team on the Tuesday. He broke the news to me saying the selectors didn't think I was going well. They had a strong enough case, in fairness, but I was still devastated.

I took it on the chin. I could see his point of view at the time but I still felt that I'd done enough in big games to go with me because I felt fellas who would have been getting 'my' place … I felt I was in a better position.

But again, I wasn't one for throwing the toys out of the pram. I totally respected his decision. I obviously would have preferred if he had picked the team and done a Jim Gavin – basically name a side and if you must change it on the day of the match, do that.

For the record, I did pass the fitness test the night before the game out in Dunboyne, where we were staying. But the die was cast.

I didn't even get on to the pitch for the match and had to watch Dublin beat Kerry. Tommy Walsh and myself were warming up the whole day but weren't brought on.

At the banquet that night, I went into a quiet corner and kept to myself. That would have been my 10th All-Ireland decider. Maybe this is the confidence or self-delusion you need to succeed in sport, but I strongly felt I could have done something in that game to merit an inclusion.

Éamonn went on his instincts and he felt I wasn't going well and that was his prerogative. He approached me afterwards and said words to the effect of, 'Marc, you had the run-in from hell coming up to the final.'

It's hard to argue with that but I still felt that on big days like that, I could have done something for him. But it wasn't to be.

After that experience, I was weighing up whether I should carry on at all. If I was to go again, the next time I'd be playing, I'd be 36. I called my brother Fergal, whose advice was always wise, to talk things through and he summed it up, 'Jesus, you can't go out like that. You have to try and get back; that's no way to leave it and your body's in good shape.'

And it was in general. Yes, I tore my hamstring, but that would have been very unlike me. I was very lucky with injuries throughout my career.

I said to Fergal, 'You know what, you're right. I will have to give it another go.'

I felt my body was okay and that was something that I always took pride in. I decided to come back again for 2016.

CHAPTER 26

END OF THE LINE

My 36th birthday is one I won't forget. I woke up in Dublin on what was the 100-year anniversary of the Easter Rising and there was a huge commemoration planned for Croke Park.

We were to face the Dubs in the National League decider and as someone interested in Irish history, I was glad to be a part of the day. I was very patriotic and this was a huge occasion for me given it was my birthday and this special anniversary.

But things weren't long going wrong for me.

Dublin hammered us 2–18 to 13 points and I was given a tough day out chasing Bernard Brogan, despite an encouraging start. Bernard beat me out the gate that day, scoring four points and setting up a goal for Eric Lowndes.

I made a few mistakes I wouldn't usually make. A high ball came in and it should have been mine all day long.

But I got up for it and Bernard came along, tapped it away and got possession. He moved it on and the Dubs got in for a goal. If I'd just palmed it down to myself and got out, we would have avoided that.

There were a few things that I could have done better throughout the afternoon and I was disappointed. Aidan O'Mahony was dismissed too and we were chasing shadows against a team in their pomp.

But we weren't set up to succeed either.

The following day there was a funeral in Milltown Castlemaine and we went into Mike Larkin's afterwards. I leant against the bar counter and picked up the *Irish Independent* which Tomás wrote for at the time. I couldn't believe what I saw.

The back page had a blurb for Tomás's column which seemingly called out myself and Aidan, saying Éamonn Fitzmaurice is going to have to make a decision on Marc or O'Mahony. My own brother!

I lost the plot altogether. I rang Tomás and I said, 'What the fuck are you at? Whatever chance I have of keeping my place, I'll have none if you're going to be writing shite like this.'

Tomás said, 'Look, they put their own spin on the heading. Read the article.' I did and it suggested I 'wasn't at the races'.

My point to Tomás was that he made Éamonn's job a lot easier.

Tomás throwing his own brother under the bus gave Éamonn an easy option to go with when he had to make a few changes, and – surprise, surprise – that's exactly what happened.

For the start of the championship, I was sitting down.

It had all been going so well in the league. The panel was continuing to evolve. You had players like Brian Ó Beaglaoich coming in; you'd Mark O'Connor who was training. Barry Dan O'Sullivan was around the place and Tom O'Sullivan. You had all these newer players coming in.

I came back in against Down in the third game of the campaign and it went well and Kerry were motoring nicely. I was feeling optimistic for the year. *Hey, I might just go out on top here.*

We travelled up to Mayo in the fifth game and I went up the field and scored with the left leg and the body felt good. The league is, as they say, the league; but things were looking good – Donaghy was being tried out in centre field and Gooch was back in and getting game time as well.

Éamonn was trying out different things – new systems, new formations, ways of countering the sweeper which Cian O'Sullivan was bringing to a new level with Dublin. When we played Cork in the last round of the league, I got up the field again to kick a point from corner back and I did feel in great shape.

We had such a good campaign that we made the National

League semi-final and beat Roscommon comprehensively, 3–15 to 14 points. Again, I'd got up the field and kicked a point, with a now trademark dummy solo. We were looking good for the National League final, which would be played on 24 April 2016, the day I'd turn 36.

When the championship came around, I was very much outside the circle of trust. It didn't feel great and the bit that hurt the most was the fact that I genuinely felt I could do something for the team. But Éamonn went with Shane Enright, Mark Griffin and Killian Young.

I came off the bench in the first couple of games in Munster but it's nearly impossible to change anything or make an impact as a defender, especially when it's late on in the game.

For the Munster final against Tipperary, I didn't come on at all. All I could do was train away, but I knew an opportunity to really make a claim to a spot was precious. Unless you're absolutely outstanding in training it's tough to make an argument.

A week before the All-Ireland quarter-final with Clare, Ellen gave birth to a little boy. We decided to name him Tadhg Michael Ó Sé after his grandfathers, two great men.

One game at a time and all that but, in that emotional time, I find myself picturing All-Ireland final day and the chance to bring Tadhg and his big sister Alice up the steps in Croke Park to lift Sam. Every player has something that motivates them and this became mine: one last win for my young family.

It rarely works out as you envisage, does it? In the All-Ireland semi-final against Dublin with the game slipping away, Éamonn sent me on and took off the scoring threat of Paul Geaney. The Kerry public may have been puzzled by the call but I knew Éamonn wanted me to get on the ball and tear up the field like I had in the past at similar points of the championship.

Al Pacino's *Any Given Sunday* speech is a staple in team rooms and a bit of cliché now. But his game of inches mantra did come to mind late in that game and in my lost moments on the Croke Park pitch. Throughout my career I can pinpoint moments where the ball had hopped our way or another when it had bounced theirs.

David Gough was the ref that day and he saw Peter Crowley get absolutely blindsided. The referee allowed the play to continue rather than award a free in, which Bryan Sheehan would have put over the bar – it would've meant we'd drawn the match.

Instead, Dublin came down the field and Diarmuid Connolly scored *that* dream point off the left leg. And there lies my final ever game for Kerry. And I realised it too, standing on the pitch.

By then living in Tralee, Kieran Donaghy chauffeured me to training one evening and could see I needed a gee-up that particular night. There's no better man to give you a motivational speech but the fact I needed it at all wasn't my style.

I needed to get a chance to show what I could do and I wasn't getting that opportunity. I knew the writing was on the wall and there was nothing anybody could tell me that I didn't know myself in that situation, despite Donaghy's kind words, high fives and various Michael Jordan quotes. It was tough because that certainly wasn't the way that I wanted to finish up.

In my mind's eye, I gave my family one last memorable day and would finish at the top.

But there are very few people who get to do it the way they want to do it.

Declan O'Sullivan did it in 2014. My brother, Darragh did in 2009. Peter Canavan did it. Not me though – after all the memorable highs and lows, my career petered out.

I told the manager I had my mind made up more or less straight away. We were in Mallow coming down on the train and I caught him: 'Look Éamonn, that's me. I'm done. I'll leave it lie for a while, but I'm done. I can touch base with you in a few weeks.'

I think he was surprised at the timing but he said, 'Fair enough, Marc, we'll chat soon.' Éamonn, of course, had this interest in how the mighty All Blacks operated. He often cited their famous 'no dickheads' policy.

We'd discussed various mantras and practices they espoused – you leave the dressing room the way you found it; if a player is not happy with management he speaks with the manager and irons out the issues. I felt I didn't get a fair crack at the whip in my final season. One night during the season at the team hotel, I said to my roommate, Darran O'Sullivan, 'You know, Éamonn keeps on talking about not wanting any dickheads in our dressing room. You know what, Darren? I think Éamonn himself is acting a small bit of a dickhead here,' I joked.

We had day two of a meet-up after our championship exit and met in Tom Quane's, a lovely pub in Blennerville, the day after the All-Ireland semi-final. I got chatting to Éamonn and I told him straight on.

'I totally agree with your mantra of no dickheads, Éamonn,' I said, 'but as I said to Darran, I thought you were kind of being a bit of a dickhead yourself.'

In fairness, he just broke down laughing.

It was nothing personal but I felt that Tomás made Éamonn's job a lot easier then by sitting me down.

Aidan continued with that role as a sweeper and, taking nothing away from Aidan, but I felt if there was anyone who could have done a job in a sweeping role, I had the experience and the tools to do that.

But there were absolutely no sour grapes on my behalf on how I finished up. I just felt that I had something more to give in the last few games from a starting position, because in terms of fitness, I was still amongst the strongest. I know I was 36, but you see players now in different codes and they keep going until far older than that.

To go out the way I did stung a bit – losing a game to Dublin by a couple of points. That's really disappointing.

After the game, I went into the dressing room and I realised that Ellen had brought Tadhg and Alice into us. We went back out on to the field. I would have loved to have gone out onto the field with my jersey, but I'd taken it off and it had disappeared.

We walked out together to a patch of grass that had been a huge part of my life – some of the best memories of my life, that I'll go back to between now and the end of my time, played out on that piece of real estate.

It was lovely to share that moment together – for them to remember. It would have been nicer to win and be in an All-Ireland final, but you can't write the script in sport or life.

Donaghy was out on the field too with his daughter, Lola Rose, and people were speculating then was he going as well. As it turned out, he'd stick around.

I'm not a sentimental person generally and as emotionally stunted as the next Irishman, but that moment was poignant. As we kicked a ball between us in front of the empty stands, I thought of the people who came before me and got me to that pitch too.

*

I knew that was the end of the line for me and, as I've said, I told Éamonn straight away as we were literally hopping off a train. A nice metaphor.

Retirement is a shock to the system. I'd been working towards being a Kerry footballer since I was a *garsún*. Then I was part of that inner circle for all my adult life. My identity was wrapped up in that jersey and my whole lifestyle was geared towards performing on the biggest days for the team.

Then, *go tobann*, it's all over. For me, it didn't really hit home for a while.

The following year, at the start of the National League campaign, I was driving through Tralee on the way to do the big shop. It was a lovely evening and passing Austin Stack Park, the Kerry lads were heading in for training.

It's like the final scene in *Goodfellas* when Henry Hill is in witness protection and he's trying to wrap his head around a life without action. 'Now, it's all over,' and that's the hardest part.

Seeing the group come together as they hopped out of their cars and greeted each other before going in to kick ball for 90 minutes – with a goal at the end of the week – *that*'s when it hit home.

I said to Ellen, 'Wouldn't it be lovely to go training this evening,' but that part of my life was over. Then you realise how lucky you were to have that life in the first place.

*

Though I told Éamonn straight away, I announced the retirement on Dara Ó Cinnéide's Raidió na Gaeltachta show *An Saol Ó Dheas* some time later.

I think Dara had appreciated the fact that Tomás and Darragh let people know about their respective retirements on his show. He's always been a brilliant friend and team-mate to us and is such an important ambassador for the Gaeltacht.

Little did I realise at the time that it was such a big deal. And not necessarily because of me – but, unlike when top players like Tomás and Darragh called it quits, my departure marked the end of an era in people's eyes.

It was billed as the end of a long line of Ó Sés, a dynasty as one of the newspapers described it. Don MacMonagle, the well-known Kerry photographer, asked me to go back to the railway station in Blennerville and before I knew what was happening, I was posing on the disused train track. The back of the papers the following day had the headline, 'End of the line for the Ó Sés'.

Páidí was there from 1975 to 1986. Darragh, on board from the early 1990s, was in the next team that won the All-Ireland in 1997. Tomás came along next and I overlapped to stretch our presence to 2016. The last of the Mohicans. And the end of Ó Sés winning All-Irelands. For a while at least, *le cúnamh Dé*.

That pang I felt when I saw the likes of Donaghy and all the Kerry lads heading in for training? It's eased now.

When your generation goes, I find, it becomes easier. I love watching Kerry games now and going to matches with my gang and cheering them on.

I'm a supporter now again and it's lovely, but, Jesus, it was very tough back at the start of the retirement when I was almost mourning what I'd lost.

It doesn't last forever. I saw Páidí deal with the afterlife of being a player and then grappling with having the Kerry manager's job taken from him so unceremoniously. It takes some dealing with – but life goes on, of course.

I've seen other players struggle with retirement. The comfort blanket of the routine is pulled from under you; all of a sudden, I wasn't accountable to the Kerry team.

It's liberating but there's danger there. For a while there I'd admit the diet wouldn't have been the best. You must be careful because it obviously takes a hold on certain people and they don't do well with retiring. There's a scaffolding constructed around you for so long and overnight it's dismantled.

I saw that – I had so much structure and was part of a group – and now there was no accountability. I knew I had to fill the void.

No complaints. But I'm not sure people appreciate the amount of time an inter-county player puts into the game. It's different in a county like Dublin, but, for us, training in the evening was an hour back the road to Killarney, training for two hours all in, maybe there's a meeting for an hour and then it was an hour home.

Weekends, of course, could be a bus journey to Omagh or Castlebar or somewhere for a game, maybe a stay overnight. The few days would be gone and then you'd be back into work.

I'd imagine Ellen, understandably, thought that when I retired from Kerry that she'd get me all to herself and it'd be a little bit of payback time. Little did we know.

Conall Ó Cruadhlaoich was asked to be manager of An Ghaeltacht, he was three years older and a great friend. He was clever at the time – knowing I'd retired from Kerry, he approached me about being joint An Ghaeltacht manager.

He saw it as a way of really getting me on board because if I was newly retired from the inter-county scene and living in Tralee an hour away from the club … was I really going to give the commitment to An Ghaeltacht?

Now he had an opportunity to make me joint manager or more accurately 'player/joint manager'. I definitely bought in. It really came at the right time for me and we went on a brilliant, enjoyable adventure together. We ended up getting to an All-Ireland semi-final against Moy, one step away from a return to that Croke Park pitch.

I'd won my first intermediate medal in 1998 and then went on and played senior with An Ghaeltacht, earning my first senior county championship title in 2001, and then another senior county championship in 2003.

Though I'd won my first intermediate in 1998, my second came in 2017. It was a lovely way to bookend things. We got as far as Thurles and Moy beat us in the last few minutes of the game. But the whole experience was good for the soul.

When you retire, you go back with the club and people might say the standard isn't the same. It certainly isn't, but at the time we had a very good An Ghaeltacht team and we had a team that was challenging for the intermediate and then we had young players coming through.

We had a raft of young lads who won Hogan Cup titles with Chorca Dhuibhne. And working with these fellas was a tonic. I really enjoyed that, and it was important that I had something like that to fall back on.

After my retirement, the chatter then was 'Who was the best Ó Sé?' I thought it was completely unfair to be seeing who was the best because we were all completely different players. I don't think Darragh could have played in the full back line and none of us, only him, could have played midfield the way he did.

Each was good at what they did and an important thing is timing; I consider myself hugely lucky to have played when I did. When I came along, I came onto a Kerry team that was extremely good.

I look at the likes of Maurice Fitzgerald and he was on a poor Kerry team in the early 1990s and the chances of winning an All-Ireland were slim.

But I was in the right place at the right time and came on board as Kerry were winning All-Irelands again. They won an All-Ireland in 2000 under Páidí and we got to the final in 2002, in my first year.

Then getting the win in 2004 was huge and that was something that I wanted to do again and again and again. You could never get enough of that. So, it's easier to have a great career and look a good player when you plug into a system that's already humming. I was lucky enough to win five All-Irelands but I also lost six; five with Kerry and one with An Ghaeltacht.

I'd take that return on a career any day of the week, although the club final defeat was a huge loss. Because you see fellas who tried so hard to win All-Irelands and couldn't get over the line or they might be supremely talented players and work as hard and intelligently as anyone in Kerry and Dublin – but because they play for a particular county, they won't ever get the chance to earn a Celtic Cross.

The likes of Declan Browne and David Tubridy come to mind and there were lots more like that who gave me so many headaches over my time. I'm self-aware enough to understand that geography and timing are so important in our games in particular. I'm self-aware enough to understand that.

CHAPTER 27

THE INVISIBLE STRING

I'd stand behind the bar in Páidí's over the years and a former opponent of his would come in through the door. It happened a lot. A middle-aged man, holding the door open for his wife and immediately scanning the bar for a former foe.

Páidí would, of course, offer a warm welcome and they'd sit for a while catching up and before long, reminiscing. Two lions in winter.

There was a strong bond between Páidí and his vintage with the lads from Cork, Dublin, Offaly and all around the country. I hope I'll sit down with the lads I faced down in the years ahead too. I learned enough from them.

Players like Michael Meehan were a nightmare. Whether I want to or not, I often think of the 2004 club final and our efforts to stop him. Often the best approach was to try to stem the momentum before it gained pace. He'd play this game of chicken with his markers where he'd run at you at pace and then put on the brakes suddenly and then he'd have his shot. It was highly effective. I've gotten to know Michael well now through our work on GAA+ and we often talk about our encounters. I don't think he realises what a force he was when he ran at you. Maybe he did, but I certainly knew what I was up against when he was on the field.

Mike Frank Russell did that to great effect as well. He'd drum down a flank, put on the brakes, turn on the other foot and bang – over the bar.

When I first started training with the Kerry senior panel around 2000, Mike Frank was an All Star and Kerry won the All-Ireland. I was raw and trying to make my way and served an apprenticeship marking Mike Frank in those training games. I built a career on that induction.

It brought me along tonnes in terms of defending one-on-one. I was never afraid of that later because of those early battles, watching those players.

I look back and feel just so lucky to have played with the players I played with and to have the friends I made both playing against and playing with.

Something I learned watching some of the game's greats pass through our crossroads, and later from my corner of the dressing room, is that your time will come and go. You're only minding the jersey for someone who'll come after you.

Because of the work of those wearing the shirt, the different numbers have become iconic.

If I think about the No 8, my mind conjures up Mick O'Connell fielding a high ball, I think of Jack O'Shea and I think of Darragh, continuing that tradition in the Kerry midfield.

The No 14 evokes Bomber Liston and Kieran Donaghy afterwards.

I wore the No 2 mainly throughout my career. It was the number I was always very proud of and I just think of Páidí wearing it when he moved from No 5 back to No 2. That meant something to me.

Ógie Moran made No 11 his own. Declan then took hold of it afterwards. Seánie O'Shea now has it. These numbers are a connection through the generations. And you want to keep up the high standards that have been set by the people who've passed it on.

It's like the No 7 at Man United – Best, Robson, Cantona, Beckham, Ronaldo.

Many people know that no Kerry skipper has ever won an All-Ireland with the No 13 on their back. These *piseogs* are taken seriously here and it's why they change David Clifford from No 13 to No 14 when he's captain of Kerry.

Another superstition related to where you sat in the

dressing room. Jack O'Connor once remarked that myself and Galvin were always down the back of the room for meetings – like two bold lads.

On the bus the likes of Donaghy would be down the back of the bus, but I'd be kind of halfway down. That was my spot always. It gave me the chance for a quick getaway. Say, if you were coming to Croke Park in through the tunnel the cameras would be waiting at the top of the bus. You'd be able to cut out the side door, get your bag in the side and slip in the dressing room. When we used to get to Croke Park or some other ground, the bus would stop and I'd have to roar from halfway down: 'Side door!' Everyone would laugh at what became a catchphrase. That was my seat then.

It had its disadvantages as well. If you had a long journey and you were up to Donegal and some fella's belly mightn't have been the best he'd go into the toilet and you'd know all about it.

Barry John Keane would have come on the scene around 2011. Talk about a character.

He trains the underage team above with Strand Road now and all my buddies around the club say that Barry John is brilliant with the underage players – probably because he's a kid himself.

In 2013, we lost the first four games at the start of Éamonn Fitzmaurice's reign and he was under pressure.

We were making the long trip back from Donegal after another shocking performance. No one was talking on the bus; the mood was not good.

You could tell too that, naturally, Éamonn was at the end of his tether nearly. The chat was intense.

Donegal had beaten us 1–12 to 0–6. It was shocking stuff altogether and you're wondering what's going on here?

I got injured that same day above there, shipping a very heavy tackle in the second half. It was going to be a long spin home on the bus.

Barry John seemed oblivious to the atmosphere. His loud, infectious laugh was rolling down the aisle from the back seat, where he was sitting with Donaghy.

Every few miles the silence was broken with this loud 'HAHAHAHA!' It was crazy.

This distinctive guffaw went up every now and then as we were wending our way down through the length of the country. From my perch in the middle of the bus, I looked up to the front and I looked back at Barry John and said, 'Jesus Christ, Fitzmaurice is going to blow a head gasket here.'

I texted Donaghy, saying, 'Will you talk to that young fella before all hell breaks loose, please, big man?'

And Donaghy writes back, 'Yeah, man, I've done it already.' A thumbs-up emoji too.

I replied, 'Big Fella' – I call Donaghy the big fella – 'honestly, Fitzmaurice will lose the plot here.'

And he said, 'What else can I do?'

Next thing, there's another big Fargo Boyle laugh from the back of the bus. Well, my God – Fitzy stormed down the aisle to the back of the bus and he absolutely reddened Barry John. We were all staring ahead, afraid to exhale. That was the last involvement Barry John had with the Kerry team for that year. Nice knowing you, kid.

Paddy Andrews told me in his first year with the Dubs that Pat Gilroy came in; he said he was taking the piss, not doing the stuff he needed to be doing, just being a bit immature. Pat apparently just came to him in the nicest possible way and he said, 'Look, we must let you go. You're not what we want at the moment. If you change your ways, you'll be back in.'

That was very much the way with Barry John.

It's like Morgan Freeman in the *Shawshank Redemption* when he's thinking back to his youth and saying, 'I look back on the way I was then: a young, stupid kid who committed that terrible crime. I want to talk to him. I want to try to talk some sense to him, tell him the way things are. But I can't. That kid's long gone, and this old man is all that's left.'

Sometimes you have to learn the hard way. Barry John will look back on that incident and say it helped him because he came back the following year in 2014 and he was outstanding.

So much so that I used to even ask Fitzmaurice to put me on Barry John because what I would find is that over and back, that agility that he had, he would train you to become better. He brought a huge amount to the team – and was a brilliant character on those long journeys.

I'm in a WhatsApp that's generously called, The Legends.

There's Alan Brogan, Anthony Daly, Jackie Tyrell, Dessie Dolan, Mick Galwey, Conor 'Sketches' Moore, Johnny 'Long Hall' Kennedy, Paddy Magee. What a gang. The day after the Dublin five in a row, we woke up and Shane Lowry had been added to the group.

Someone is always hopping a ball in the chat.

I used to come back to Ceann Trá and cut the grass for my mother during Covid. And of course it worked out well that I was then able to go over for my couple of pints afterwards in Páidí's when pints were hard to come by.

I remember taking a video of cutting the lawn next to Galwey's house and putting it up in the group and Galwey texting me back, 'Marco, would you ever fire a stone in through my window so it'd give me an excuse to go down there?'

A lot of the chat from the hurling fraternity in the group is not complimentary about football. I think that has changed now with Jim Gavin and the FRC's (Football Review Committee) new rules – that's quietened the talk from the hurling fellas in the group somewhat. I think the reimagining of the game has been brilliant and I've been buzzing watching games full of chaos and old-school skill.

I can see my brother Darragh thriving in midfield in this era with the reintroduction of high fielding in midfield. So too, I'd love a go again. Far from just being about forwards, this new game is finally returning the art to the skill of one-on-one defending.

Towards the fag end of my career, defending became an exercise in painting by numbers. Where before I'd try to imitate my full back idols like John O'Keeffe and make proper interventions, now we were instructed to shadow attackers and play a percentage game.

There can be no going back to that.

Pull back the trench coat and every sports squad is made up of a series of cliques. Throughout my time with Kerry, we always had lots of little factions.

It's a vast county with distinct areas so maybe it was natural that oftentimes we'd fall into groups along those lines of latitude and longitude.

Even going back as far as Páidí's time there was a thing where the West Kerry and the North Kerry fellas seemed to get on. There's a wildness in the west that's matched by north Kerry.

It was always very much myself, Tomás and Darragh, naturally, with our friend and clubmate Dara Ó Cinnéide, Aodán Mac Gearailt, Finuge's Paul Galvin and his brother-in-law, Éamonn Fitzmaurice.

That seemed to be the core group for me.

Prior to that, Darragh and Ó Cinnéide lived in north Kerry, where the former worked at the ESB and the latter worked with Kerry Group. They both lived in Tarbert and would have been trucking around with the likes of Éamonn Breen and Liam O'Flaherty.

Páidí had gone to school there, in exile, and my mom and dad had lived there. There was very much a connection to north Kerry. That's not to say that we weren't friendly with anyone else. Jeez, that wasn't the case at all.

But when I think back now and reflect on my time, were we ever really that close?

I respect them all and have fondness for the times we shared and gratitude that we were able to do it. Do I text many of the Kerry players? Am I friendly with many Kerry players? I'd consider myself good friends with six or seven.

My own brothers aside, I'd be particularly friendly with Galvin. I got him the present of a gramophone for his wedding and it's nice to get a video some evenings of a vinyl on the turn table. I'm good pals still with Séamus Moynihan and Brosnan around the town. I keep in contact with Gooch and Darran O'Sullivan – but it's with the same frequency and fluency that your typical 40-something Irishmen communicate.

Are we good for keeping in contact as a group? I think it's too early to tell. Now, we're not long off the treadmill, lots of us have young kids and life is busy. We haven't hit the time for jubilee gatherings or anniversaries. So hopefully we'll come back together in the years ahead.

If there's a golf day, I don't get the chance to tee it up. We all have full-time jobs; we're involved in training teams and running around the place after children.

But I know if I was stuck for something or needed a dig out, I could call on any of the lads and I'd like to think they'd be there at the drop of a hat. I hope they realise I'd be there for them at the end of the phone too. We soldiered together long enough and that bond is strong.

There's a nice spot for coffee in Tralee inside in the train station run by Ellen McElligott and her two sons, Mike and Eoin. I was making my morning pit-stop on the way to work one morning recently and bumped into Aidan O'Mahony.

Ellen, a right character, saw us both coming before we saw each other and kindly stood us both our coffees. We hung around in the car park for half an hour catching up after, falling back into the familiar chat, like we still see each other every Tuesday and Thursday evening and each weekend.

We were always great pals and that man would've gone through the wall for any of us. The conversation was good for the soul. Afterwards in school I glanced at my phone and saw a text from Aidan: 'Great to catch up. We don't do it enough.'

And he's right. We don't. It's easy to let it drift.

You're always curious about how it was on the other side. Some of the Dublin lads of our vintage tell me that the Dubs team were all mates. Maybe they were all of a similar generation and background; all grew up within 30 minutes of each other. It was different with us.

The whole thing around Kerry was a bit of a circus at times too. It became the centre of a social hub where the wives and girlfriends were all involved and to me, it needed to be more player-driven. I don't think it was at times.

I heard Darren say recently that the team he finished up on were not even a quarter as good as the team of my era – but the difference was they were all teammates. By implication, we weren't.

But I would go so far as to say that with Páidí's team there were cliques, throughout the 1970s and the 1980s.

In that great team they had the so-called Rat Pack: Páidí, Eoin Liston, Seánie Walsh, Ógie Moran and they'd come back west after a Munster final and they'd tour west Kerry for maybe four days, like Sinatra and Dean Martin up and down the Las Vegas Strip.

In those days, Micko wasn't expecting you back in until maybe a Thursday night. If even.

The Heavy Gang, as Micko knew them, would come back west and tour around listening to music and meeting people, hitting places like Johnny Frank's in Ballydavid, An Bothar in Cuas, half of Dingle.

The famous caravan in the cross would be a hostel of sorts in the time after a Munster final.

Beatrice would provide a tray of sandwiches when the group landed back at the end of the night and the following morning they'd wake to the smell of her cooking a fried breakfast.

I was too young to remember but I know my older brothers would get a thrill from peeking inside to see some of the Kerry stars – gods to the likes of us – stretching out their legs inside in this old caravan.

As well as that tight unit, there was probably another South Kerry group, plus a Tralee bunch.

It's a big county; if I was to go down to south Kerry, it'd take me the bones of an hour and a half.

It's the same for everyone. Unless you were living in Tralee or Killarney, everyone would have had a trek going to training. It would be an hour and a bit for us – and longer at the height of the summer with the traffic – and the same back.

But we loved the fun of the West Kerry car, as we called it, but it lent itself to a kind of a clique in its own way as well.

Páidí came out of a lift in the team hotel one morning when he was Kerry manager and the three of us brothers plus Dara Ó Cinnéide and Aodán Mac Gearailt were lounging around in the lobby drinking *tae*.

At the time we had won the county championship and it was natural to have a group of players from the champions' team. But Páidí came strutting through the lobby and said, 'Jesus Christ, lads will ye fucking spread out around the place before I lose my job. They'll think that there's no one else only An Ghaeltacht players.'

Maybe we should have mingled a bit more.

In 2002, on the famous trip to South Africa, I went on my own but plenty of the lads brought wives and girlfriends, which was great.

But Páidí insisted that at the end of the trip, the so-called WAGS went home – three days early. He wanted the players just to be together as a unit.

I thought it was a great idea because there was that period of time when we had the sense that we were just there with each other. Before that, when we lost in 2001 to Meath in the semi-final Páidí brought us off to New York for five nights – just the team, not long after the Twin Towers collapsed.

I remember going down to Ground Zero and you could still smell the smoke and see the rubble.

We were all just glued to each other on that trip and it stood to us.

We had great trips away – Australia, South Africa, Kuala Lumpur, San Francisco, Cancun in Mexico, Las Vegas. You'd be gone for two and a half weeks and at that time it worked with the calendar.

But now they've changed all that. They're gone now, I'd say, late November, very early December.

The game that we were playing, it's completely different. Now some lads are playing 12 months of the year.

I suppose we were all aware that there were groups and Jack O'Connor came in after Páidí and probably realised cliques are going to be cliques.

That's what's going to happen in teams. Jack probably wanted everyone to get on and you can totally see the merit in that, and I don't think it was a case that everyone didn't get on. We were all pally.

I used to just do my own thing and go back to west Kerry. Rarely would I go into Killarney unless it was a Munster final. But I'd always get out of Dodge around half 11 or 12. You're better off slipping away, there was always a lift back west where we could relax more.

You'd enjoy the night too, especially after a big game like a Munster final.

I was watching another game recently and there's a picture of the same game hanging in Páidí's bar – the 1998 Munster final, Cork and Kerry – Larry Tomkins' last match.

I couldn't believe the crowd that was there. Declan O'Keefe was taking the kick outs and there were people sitting on the pitch. He was tiptoeing through them to retrieve the ball before kicking it back out. Health and safety wouldn't have it today.

But the atmosphere at the game was electric. Those days are gone in terms of atmosphere.

You're walking down into the town and when the sun is beating down – that was what a real Munster final felt like. And you'd be *allowed* go for your few pints and they were the days when you would love to stay in Killarney, when you'd love to sample the atmosphere and everyone would be out on the streets and having the pint.

And I think it was probably noticed by the other players that I used to have a lift organised and I'd go back west to the haven of home.

Our generation overlapped the game's old-school days and the advent of sports science, modern methods and social media. I was watching the *American Pie* movie the other night where the fella's inside in the bedroom and he manages to send an e-mail to the lads but literally he's sending it out to the whole school.

Even if you send a private message to your friend now, or a picture to your friend, somebody, a buddy, could send it on unknowingly to another person and before you know what, the message could be in America in five minutes.

In my job, it's something we talk to our lads about the whole time. It's a whole new world out there.

Páidí went to the Netherlands to visit one of the Comórtas

Ó Sé teams not long before he passed away. Beforehand he was at home with the girls, his daughters Neasa and Siún, and they said, 'Dad, just be careful when you're over there. Take it easy, don't be drinking too much and keep the head down.'

Of course, Páidí was over there enjoying himself afterwards and there was a photograph taken of him with a pint in his hand, clearly having plenty of fun. When he came home, he was asked, 'Were you taking it easy?'

'Oh Jesus, yeah,' he insisted. And they pulled out the phone and they said, 'And who was this?'

He was completely dumbfounded. 'How did you get that? Were you there?'

That was back then – in 2012 – and the digital side of things was just ramping up then. When Fitzmaurice took charge in November 2012, he stood in front of us and said everything was changing.

Everything we were going to do was going to be on the smartphone; everything we did, we ate, the training we did, how we slept, we put it all on an app; and your training workload would be emailed to you.

Everything would be on your phone. And Tomás, just in the middle of the whole speech says, 'All that is lost on me because I've got a Nokia 6310.' The whole place erupted again.

Tomás would have been the oldest member of the team. But it was just about then that smartphones were coming in. We got the last of the old-school carry-on.

There was a Monday club then, of course, and some would even round it out with a couple of pints on the Tuesday before knuckling down again.

But that changed over the course of my career. When Éamonn Fitzmaurice came in, he'd like to get these fellas in harness again quickly. He was like the parent who did his fair share of raving in his day too. He knew all the tricks. He laid down the law and used to get us back in training on a Monday night – after a Sunday game.

And it was more just to keep us off the streets, I think. We didn't do a whole lot but he liked to get us together. He wanted our minds as much as our bodies switched back on.

Later, when the older brigade were gone and I was still fighting the good fight for that generation, he got us in on a Monday evening, after a big win on the Sunday.

It was a young Kerry team in and around 2014. The average age in the West Kerry car had dropped significantly. I started out in the back seat all those years before with Páidí throwing the thing around corners and stopping for ice cream on the way home, if he was in a good mood.

This evening, I was heading in along with my companions, Mikey and Paul Geaney and Donnchadh Walsh, who was living in west Kerry at the time. I looked into the rearview mirror and said, 'Look, lads, Éamonn's going to say here there's no drink tonight. I'm telling you though, I'm going for a few pints when we get home. I don't think it's a big deal.'

It was part of the routine.

'We're not going to do anything out of the way, just a few jars. We're not out again in championship for three weeks, it's not like it will make any difference.'

The lads were in total agreement. 'Yeah, yeah, Marc,' the boys are saying. Éamonn gave us a right speech inside in Fitzgerald Stadium the same night: we need to do this and we need to do that.

And coming out the road, all the boys had changed their tune – except of course Mikey Geaney. Mikey and myself had a couple of quiet pints.

Mikey was a great West Kerry character, great fun; I really enjoyed him. He had a good sense of humour and he was always great craic. He had a huge role to play as well in 2014. He came off the bench a few times against Mayo and started wing forward. And I thought he just brought that doggedness that you needed for a wing forward.

Plus, he was able to pop in with a few scores. His brother Paul was maturing well also and what a man to sniff a goal, just look at the All-Ireland final against Donegal. I enjoyed that team generally but it was a completely different team and vibe with not many of the older guard left.

There were the likes of myself, Gooch, O'Mahony, Donaghy, Declan O'Sullivan, Bryan Sheehan. We were the older fellas then.

CHAPTER 28

'AN POC AR BUILE'

There's the famous line from one of the Kerry Golden Years generation, surrounded by journalists at another pre-All-Ireland final press night in Killarney: 'Put me down for what I said last year.'

Páidí had a funny relationship with the media – he could be cagey and protective but at the same time, journalists loved the chance to talk to him and he was friendly with lots of reporters. He'd always said to all of us that the time to be in the papers was the Monday after a game, not the Sunday.

'I'll tell you something,' he said, 'watch these people who do these two-page spreads in the Sunday broadsheets the morning of a game.

'Just watch them,' he says, 'and you watch how they play that day.'

I go back to the time when he was Kerry skipper. He was so conscious of Kerry captains never playing well in

All-Ireland finals and he wanted to make sure that he played well. He'd make sure that he minded us and he was clever in ways. When it came to press nights and various obligations, he put the fellas that he knew didn't mind chatting away and it wouldn't affect them.

My brother Darragh didn't want to do it. He had no interest in it. Over the course of his career, he did maybe three or four big interviews. Ó Cinnéide was good at it, obviously – a great communicator and someone who has made their own career in broadcasting and journalism.

I saw one Kerry footballer recently and he did an interview that was absolutely shocking. This fella was an experienced Kerry footballer and it was clear he was nervous doing it; he wasn't comfortable and you could see the interviewer thinking I wouldn't be too confident watching you now on Sunday.

It's important fellas get experience doing this side of things too. Other sports are a lot better at trusting their players and relying on them to promote the game.

One All-Ireland media night we were all thrown into the room like it was a speed-dating thing. But Páidí caught the Gooch as he was walking in. 'No … go out there you.' Because everyone wanted to talk to the Gooch and Páidí was just protecting him. But the irony of the whole thing here was Páidí telling us not to do this or that with journalists, yet he was the best ever at using the media.

He was a genius really at marketing for his business.

Páidí created a brand behind his personality through his charisma and intelligence and ability to build relationships organically.

Páidí was a great footballer on a truly great team – a couple of great teams. He was an unbelievable footballer but his force of personality and leadership set him apart. When you talk about the best footballers, you'd point to Jack O'Shea, Pat Spillane, Mikey Sheehy. But if you asked the man on the street to name a player from the great Kerry team of the 1970s or 1980s … would 9 out of 10 say Páidí first?

He is amongst the most famous players in our game's history. A big part of that was his achievements on the pitch. Another part was because he put himself out there.

But that was Páidí. If he saw Tomás tear up the wing and fire over a point, he'd be roaring at him to mind the No 5 spot like he was told. But we'd think back to the 1982 final against Offaly, probably Páidí's best game, and one we knew well from the VHS tapes. He went up the field from the same position and kicked two points.

Maybe he knew with experience that when he was going up the field – even if he did kick a point or two – we were more open at the back, but he was a gas man.

He could be shy too.

If you look at the pictures hanging around the pub at Ard an Bhóthair, you'll see a nice collection in the corner of his 21st birthday. There's my father, Uncle Tom, grandparents, neighbours and a bishop, and Páidí is well turned out in a new wide-lapel suit and fashionably loud shirt and tie.

But you can see the shyness in him. You can detect the same quality in the footage with Dolly Parton in the pub as he struggles to maintain eye contact with this larger-than-life music star. But he always admitted himself he was shy.

When he was in the right company, he was totally at ease and full of his swagger and charisma and completely central to things. But, jeez, if he knew his company, if he knew who he was with, there was no shyness, just this vibrant character who lit the place up – and the craic we would have.

The day of the 2009 All-Ireland final, we were in The Boar's Head and someone asked him to sing. A supporter had written a song about Gooch and Tomás and the drinking episode.

> Ó Sé and Cooper are super at knocking back the pints.
> When Jack O'Connor got the news, his heart had nearly stopped.

And someone asked him to sing the song, so he pulled out his reading glasses and made an attempt at it. People loved it, of course.

Páidí had no concept of what YouTube or Facebook or social media was. He just didn't know about it or how things worked. A few weeks went by and someone in the bar said to him, as Páidí served up their pint, 'You were brilliant singing that song about the Gooch and Tomás.'

He was completely shocked to discover this thing was up online, clocking up plenty of views. A couple of weeks later, Cór Cúil Aodha from Cork were inside in Dingle during the regatta and they were singing a few sean-nós songs in Dick Mack's – scene of the crime for Tomás and I going back to 2009, of course.

The lads in the choir turned to Páidí – who was with some friends, like some of the Haughey family – and they started 'An Poc ar Buile'. They called Páidí for the next verse *as Gaeilge*.

Someone in the bar just innocently took out their phone to text someone or just check the time and Páidí jumped up and said, 'Hey, there's no YouTube on that, is there?' We all laughed.

But he was at ease in that place, in that company and there was no shyness there because it was his turf and he knew the people. Nowadays I feel sorry for players and what they have to deal with. I don't know how they can have any down time or peace together with the preponderance of phones.

I'm thankful we avoided the worst of that. We probably wouldn't have survived long.

Throughout my career, Mícheál Ó Muircheartaigh was a constant presence. He was a link back to west Kerry too.

He'd always call into the dressing room before games and would stand by the door and chat to anyone who passed. He might be picking up bits of information that would inform his colourful commentary or just catching up with people for its own sake. Páidí would be uptight before big games and Mícheál would give a nod and Páidí would tersely salute, 'Hi, Mícheál,' and go about his own business.

Mícheál knew well to stay out of Páidí's way in those moments. Páidí just did his own thing, did what he had to do and Mícheál appreciated that. But he called into all the dressing rooms; it wasn't just a Kerry thing.

The first time I met him I was working in Kingdom Fresh, a fruit and veg shop in Dingle, which supplied all the pubs and restaurants around the area. It was owned by Seán and Breda Duffy. Breda was a daughter of Mick Murphy, from Ventry, who won an All-Ireland with Kerry. Seán, meanwhile, was a proud Mayo man from Louisburgh. I remember when Kerry played Mayo in the All-Ireland semi-final in 1996. Seán rostered me to work at the time of the match and I told him I quit. He just laughed and welcomed me back for my next shift after I returned from seeing the game in Dublin.

He was a teacher back in Cill Mhic an Domhnaigh. Later we had Bean Uí Geaney, the grandmother of Paul and Michael Geaney. We're all connected.

I was working away at my summer job and Mícheál came in. He just looked around and said, '*Mála* Golden Wonders.'

So, I got the bag and said, '*Sé punt, le do thoil,*' or whatever the price was.

He looked at me and says, in that distinctive voice, '*Cuir ar do ghualainn iad* [Put it on your shoulder].' A 13-year-old under a bag of potatoes, I followed him out to his Toyota – he always had Toyotas. He didn't let on he knew who I was even if he asked me where I came from. Once you say Ard an Bhóthair, it's a fair guess you're an Ó Sé.

He opened the boot, thanked me and I threw in the bag. The next time we'd meet would be in Croke Park. It wasn't carrying a bag of spuds, but I asked him much later if he'd do *me* a favour.

We were organising a fundraiser for our school, CBS The Green, to try to get some money together for an astro pitch. We were chasing people to take part in this game The Cube and I asked Mícheál to come to the launch, which he did.

I said, 'Look, the school will put you up; there's a budget put aside.'

'No, no,' *as Gaeilge*, 'I'm driving back again tonight. We're flying out to Australia in the morning with the International Rules.'

I could not believe this.

I said, 'What time is the flight?'

'*Cúig a clog ar maidin* [Five in the morning].'

He wouldn't have got into his car until at least 10 p.m., leaving Tralee, and the flight was at 5 a.m. from Dublin airport.

After Páidí died, my uncle Tom, Tom Crowley, Mícheál and some other great men formed a committee to raise funds to erect a statue in memory of him. It's a shrine to people now at Ard an Bhóthair. Again, Mícheál couldn't do enough for us. That's the kind of pedigree that you had – a lovely man.

Mícheál knew too that his words carried a lot of weight and he carried that responsibility so well. He painted a beautiful picture of what was playing out in front of him but was always so positive.

I think Mícheál Ó Sé from our club, who was superb on local radio, was the same.

That generation were all the same school of thought. They knew the people who were listening.

I'll always remember a game Mícheál was commentating on, which I witnessed from his vantage point. Our buddy J.J. Corduff got badly injured in a Comórtas Peile na Gaeltacht match. I was going home with Mícheál afterwards so I was standing by the gantry, which would have been unusual for me.

As I was loitering by the broadcast position, J.J. broke his leg in the middle of the pitch. But Mícheál was on the radio speaking, *as Gaeilge*, saying '*Nil se ró-olc* [It's not too bad].'

'*Tá sé ceart go leor* [He's okay].'

And next thing he got off air and I said to him, 'Mícheál, J.J.'s in a bad way. What were you saying there?'

'Marc,' he explained, 'J.J.'s mother Cathy is at home

listening to this. I don't want to put her under stress.' I just thought, *This man is incredible* – and it was a good lesson to me.

I think Mícheál Ó Sé and Mícheál Ó Muircheartaigh were very similar in the way they thought and the way they knew their audience, too. You look now and it's changed and is harder.

CHAPTER 29

THE JERSEY

People ask me now what type of manager or coach I am. I was lucky throughout my career to experience different types of coaches who brought different values and skills to the job.

I'd like to think I kept my eyes open throughout and mentally bookmarked what I liked and circled the stuff I didn't. I'm not very dogmatic – I don't have a hard and fast philosophy on how I like to play or how my teams should line out.

I want to play good football. That's what we were reared on in west Kerry. But then you must realise what type of footballers you have and what type of football suits them best. To paraphrase an old friend, Anthony Daly, 'If you've no paint, you can't paint.'

If you have a certain type of a footballer, you can play a certain type of a way.

With Listowel now, it's enjoyable and I love being involved with the young lads in school. The Corn Uí Mhuirí is a high standard and it means so much.

Of the men I was managed by, Éamonn was excellent on culture and how we prepared. He's a natural storyteller, is empathetic and tapped into various narratives to pull us together and align us.

With Éamonn too I learned loads about analysis and how to communicate with a player when they don't see what they're doing wrong. You can show them in technicolour on video and show exactly where they're going right … and wrong.

In my time I'd be preparing to face Colm O'Neill or Donncha O'Connor of Cork and you could go on the phone, check into this bespoke app and review clips of all these players, at a time of your own convenience, when you were having your lunch or had a minute to yourself.

He brought it to a new level in terms of the specialism of it. We also had to log each day what our energy levels were like, how well we slept, our hydration. I'd imagine since I've retired that sport science has pushed on more.

With the video analysis too, if players are still not getting the message, you can call them out in front of a group. It sometimes helps them see more clearly. You have to be tough.

There's no way you're going to get anywhere unless you are tough and have that edge when it comes to it. The one thing with Páidí was he didn't give a damn who you were;

he was ruthless. He didn't care who you were. Ask Martin Flanagan, the best player in the Westmeath team, who Páidí thought needed to be dropped off the panel.

He was just ruthless and he put out the best team that he felt was ready to take to the field. Listen, he dragged me off the field in my first All-Ireland final, knowing that it would be a setback for me personally.

I like to think he knew I'd be able to recover from that day. But realistically, the most important thing – the *only* thing – was winning that All-Ireland for Kerry.

Jack O'Connor was different to Páidí, God knows, in many ways. I think he had great success with Kerry over the years – and it's a lesson I noted – because he surrounded himself with good people. That's not faint praise – it takes an intelligence and confidence to do it, and you don't need to look any further than this year's great All-Ireland win to see that.

In his latest stint back in Kerry, he's got the very experienced coach Cian O'Neill in. Cian was outstanding in 2014, when I was there, and he's shown his value to the group again in helping Kerry to an All-Ireland in 2025. It will be interesting to see what happens next with what is a young, talented panel who can achieve even more.

Before that, Paddy Tally apparently had huge influence and Fitzmaurice was a very good coach and lieutenant for Jack. He was a wise choice as a conduit between the players and the manager.

I took a lot from Pat O'Shea too, probably the best coach

I've had an interaction with. And the main thing I appreciated was that he treated us like adults. With someone like Jack, you could be treated like a child or a student at times. I'm a teacher, so this isn't derogatory necessarily, but there was the touch of the *muinteoir* with Jack and us.

Whereas Pat O'Shea might have the approach that if you had a few pints, maybe a night you shouldn't have had, Pat wouldn't really say anything.

But if you played shite the following Tuesday night in training, he'd say: 'Come here: how do you think that went? Did you have a few pints on Saturday night?'

He'd come about it a different way – maybe he was more influenced by the American basketball side of things than the GAA's culture of drinking bans.

We weren't driving to a casino to blow off some steam like Michael Jordan the night before an NBA Finals game. But if we were, we just needed to back it up on the pitch.

He had his ways too, and I think I was very lucky to play under all those managers and I learned something new from all of them, and all of that helped.

Right now, I'm a coach, rather than the manager, but I'm very hands on and have hope to keep evolving. At the moment I come in and talk to the manager and we can decide what needs to be worked on.

And that's the beauty about being the coach; if there's any issues to be ironed out, the manager can do that.

I was doing that with Listry. I was the manager and I was

the man dealing with all the messages – the man doing the everything, really. Whereas when you're coaching, all you're just doing is the coaching. It's so enjoyable what I'm doing now.

I went for the Kerry minors job some time ago and thought I might be in with a good shot. It took Páidí a while to get the Kerry gig. He was knocked back in 1989 and 1992 – they say many within the county executive saw him as a loose cannon. They were right there, but he proved he was more than up to the job in the end. Who knows, maybe I'll go for it again.

Like the Vatican or Washington DC, Kerry GAA is highly political. Páidí was well able for that too and often took soundings from friends like Charlie Haughey.

He coached West Kerry (1990–91, 1993–94), UCC (1990–92) and the Kerry U21s (1992–5), winning various titles, and he convinced the county delegates that his long record as a player and what he'd shown as a manager meant they couldn't pass him over again.

So, when I was hoping to land the Kerry minors job, Tomás got the U20s gig and maybe the writing was on the wall for my chances then. Would they put two Ó Sés in charge of the minors and 20s? 'Spread out a small bit,' as Páidí said to us that morning in the hotel lobby. 'They'll think it's only An Ghaeltacht lads we have.'

Now I get to attend games as a pundit too. I enjoy studying the match footage during the week, getting a grasp of the respective teams and how they set up and then hopping into the car at the weekend to take in a game.

Heading out the door of our busy home, Ellen often says to me, 'We can swap and I'll go on telly.'

You've got to be critical but it's easier for me because I'm in a different role to a commentator. I'm just answering the questions. You must be critical – most importantly, you want to be telling the truth of what you see.

There have been times over my career when people on telly have brought people's profession or character into debates about football. I totally disagree with that.

But you want to tell the viewer your point of view. You might differ from the fellow next to you. There are certain people then who you'll be on the TV with, or a radio broadcast, and you know they're going to kind of cut across you. You must think about what you're going to say and make sure you get your point across; even if you're disrupted or somebody cuts across you, you must deliver your point.

On TV, you don't get that much time to talk. The nature of it means you're talking maybe two or three times. GAA+, as it's called now – as well as RTÉ and the GAA themselves – shipped lots of criticism because of the new platform's very existence or the fact that some games weren't shown on terrestrial TV.

Maybe I'm biased but I think it's a natural evolution. If you look at American football, they all have their own channels. It's a no-brainer. It started off with being the situation where people abroad got to watch games that they probably would not have seen. So that was great.

But like anything it evolved and now you have a situation where people are giving out because you're not showing this game or another game on RTÉ. I get that. But as a whole package RTÉ and GAA+ are now showing *way* more games than they've ever shown before. When I was growing up, you may have got a National League final but if you didn't, you would have got *The Sunday Game* that night. There were seven games that were shown each season. That was it. You had the provincial finals, semis and the final and *The Sunday Game* to keep you going. We're spoiled now and it's great for the game.

The one thing I think should happen is the hospitals and nursing homes should get access to all games. I would be fully in agreement with that, but that's above my pay scale.

People say pay-per-view goes against the ethos of the game and all that, and I just don't see it that way because I think you're trying to promote your games.

For me growing up, playing for Kerry was everything – that's all we wanted to do. I don't think that single-minded fixation is as strong in the younger generations.

For a start, there are more options now. My young lad Tadhg now plays basketball, soccer, as well as Gaelic foot-ball and he can decide on what he wants to play himself down the line. Football – *caid* – was the only sport in which we could express ourselves. Whether we wanted it or not, we didn't have the opportunity to scrum down with a rugby team or line out with a soccer side.

That passion for the jersey starts with the families; it doesn't *just* come from the player alone. Kerry have lost lots of players over the years to Australia too. That was never on the cards with a generational talent like David Clifford because knowing the Cliffords, all David was going to do was try to bring glory to Kerry.

Some of these lads who have gone could have filled the void left by my brother Darragh. When Gooch retired – a truly great forward – we managed to find David Clifford coming off the conveyor belt. But with Darragh, I'm not sure if he's ever really been completely replaced.

I was very aware of the Dingle native Mark O'Connor and how good he was in the middle of the park. He's at Geelong now and good luck to him. The pedigree is there too; great granduncle Tom 'Gega' O'Connor would have won five All-Ireland medals with Kerry back in the 1940s. Mark is the one that got away and could have had a long career *i lár na páirce* for the Kingdom.

You hear the stories about all these fellas who are going to go off to Aussie Rules and, rightly or wrongly, you'd wonder is that level of passion there to achieve your boyhood dream?

It's natural perhaps in the modern world – but it's sad

to see a tradition diluted too. I was never going to attract an Aussie Rules scout to Ard an Bhóthair because I didn't have the physical build for their game. But if there was a knock on the door, it would never have been a decision for me.

According to the mythology, Ventry Beach was the scene of an epic battle between Cú Chulainn and Dáire Donn, the King of the World. Well, we were nursed on stories of Páidí and his Kerry teammates like *they* were Na Fianna. Before Páidí, Tom Long was the one he wanted to emulate.

These were the superheroes for us. Now, of course, every Marvel movie in the extended universe is available with a couple of clicks of a remote.

I know my passion for the green and gold is in my blood. I hope that's the same for every footballer in the county but sometimes you wonder when you see people heading off to Australia. I know my love for it is part of my DNA, nevertheless.

But Kerry is football. There'll always be players coming through and a couple each year will graduate to keep our thing going. Maybe we can do more to keep lads here. But whatever happens, Kerry football will always keep striving for excellence. I've no doubt about that.

EPILOGUE

Life now is with Ellen, Alice, Tadhg and Tommy.

After managing to avoid each other through school, college and our early work life, I met Ellen properly in The Green in Tralee, the CBS, where we both still teach.

She's an amazing woman, dedicated to her family, full of energy and passionate about her career as an English teacher. She loves her work which is one of the reasons she's so good at the job.

She puts her life and soul into everything – like the dramas she'd stage with the students for years, which were excellent productions of *Sive* or *The Field* by John B. Keane.

Like me, Ellen comes from a real football family. Her father, Tadhg McGillicuddy played with Castleisland Desmonds and was a serious player in his day. He met Marian Ryan – a Tipp woman from Ardfinnan while they were both in Dublin – and they made their life in north Kerry.

Since I started seeing Ellen, they've been absolutely amazing to me. There was always such a welcome and they're a great support to us in rearing our children. They're unbelievable people. And you can see the sense of hard work that's instilled in Ellen and I can see she's trying to weave that into the kids now and maybe me too.

Ellen has been incredible and I've been very lucky to meet her. Little did I realise when I met her that I'd have Ellen's daughter, Alice, as part of my life as well. Alice is really bright, hard-working, talented and independent.

She's a brilliant big sister to Tadhg and the smallest fella Tommy. Tadhg and Alice are as thick as thieves. Alice always has a watchful eye on her two younger brothers, and minds them and keeps them safe. It's been such a privilege to be part of that young lady's life and to see her growing up.

Tadhg is half cracked. It's the Ó Sé gene coming through, Ellen suggests sometimes. He's funny and curious and a great kid. Our happiest moments are kicking a ball off the gable end of the house, competing, eager to score and laughing together.

When people see Tommy, a tough cookie, the most common refrain is: 'He's been here before.' He already has a strong personality coming through and absolutely rules the house. It'll be interesting to see what he achieves.

If Tommy dominates the house, Ellen holds the home together and drives us on.

If she wants to achieve something she'll put her mind to it and get it done. She reminds me of another great woman in a lot of ways – my grandmother, Beatrice, the woman who started it all at Ard an Bhóthair for my family. I'm very lucky that I met her.

We live in Tralee and have a nice life in a great community. The days are busy, of course, and I don't get back west to Ceann Trá as much as I'd like. But that corner of Ventry will always be home.

That place is hardwired into me. The geography, the sea, the music, the people, the football. I'm sure it's the same for everyone; you grow from the soil up. Ard an Bhóthair moulded me and when I go back there it's like plugging into a charging station – I leave again full up for another while.

Whatever our kids go on to do, they'll know where their family come from and the tradition and culture and place. I tell people I want to be buried in Ventry when the time comes, hopefully a long time in the future. But maybe we'll get back there to actually live at some stage as a family.

Playing in the back garden with my three brothers, I always imagined it as Croke Park and us as the next generation to continue our tradition. But did I think we'd actually all get there? What we experienced together was beyond even a child's most vivid dreams, I think.

Seeing Kerry win the All-Ireland this year from the

stands and witnessing what it meant to the next generation brought home how powerful it all is.

I saw Tadhg, who is just starting to understand the game, and the effect the victory had on him. Seeing the likes of the Cliffords, Seánie O'Shea and Joe O'Connor and the rest of those boys play football the way they do can't but inspire those coming after them.

Hopefully there'll always be kids in Kerry – and each county – whose imaginations are fired by these games and who dare to dream the same as me. If that's the case, the future is very bright.

As a young player, our family's footballing legacy weighed on me, but ultimately I realised it was a gift and something I tried to live up to and thrive on by playing football our way.

I was so fortunate to be able to do what I did with my brothers – for club and county – and to do my best for my uncle Páidí as my manager. All those years and everything that happened, good and bad, the winning and losing, will always be with me and I'm so grateful to have experienced it.

Tomás put it typically – and correctly – when asked to reflect on my career recently: 'He did alright,' he said with a half-smile. There's a lot folded into that reply; our relationship as brothers, the particular way we were all reared by our parents, the humility of our homeplace.

I'd like to think we all did alright and kept the thing going for those who will come after us.

Acknowledgements

I have so many people to thank and the first place to start is at home. Growing up at Ard an Bhóthair was such a happy upbringing and the people to thank for that are my mom and dad. My parents were always there for me, especially in my formative years, and I'll be forever grateful.

To my brothers, who were always in my corner too, thanks. I looked up to Fergal, Darragh and Tomás in every way and they were always there to lead the way, support me and give me advice when it was needed. On and off the field, we had each other's backs – and that will always be the case.

Thanks to my uncles, Páidí and Tom, who I was lucky to have across the road and, on my mother's side, my uncle Mike, who always looked after me. Though he's now sadly gone, Mike's wife Marion, my godmother, never forgets me still.

To my club, An Ghaeltacht, where it started and finished. All the coaches from underage up who, like so many volunteers around the country in our association, put their time into training us and looking after us throughout the years.

Special mention to Liam Ó Rócháin for helping me along the way in my early days and to Mícheál Ó Sé for always nurturing me and convincing me, as a young player, that I could go on and become a good player. In our community, he was always there, from U14, to U16, to minor, and always had that positive influence on me and, I know, many others.

To all my clubmates with An Ghaeltacht, who I am still so pally with. I soldiered with those boys all the way up and they are the fellas I feel most comfortable with even now. We shared great days down the years, and I know An Ghaeltacht will go on to make new memories for our tribe.

Thanks to all my teachers at Cill Mhic an Domnaigh and Tralee CBS and all my coaches with Kerry from U16, to minor, to U21, to senior. Amongst them was the great Mikey Sheehy, who always told me that I was destined for great things and gave me that confidence to push on and believe in myself.

To Tony O'Keefe, who was principal in Tralee CBS and gave me my start in the school and was secretary of the Kerry county board, and John O'Keeffe, a colleague of mine and also a Kerry coach, a great mentor both to me in my profession and playing for Kerry; he was so important to me as I started out with the county.

To all my colleagues in the school, CBS The Green, past and present, who've been very helpful to me through the years.

To my Kerry teammates – I wouldn't have won what I was fortunate enough to win only for the great players that sat beside me on long bus journeys and in dressing-rooms throughout our run together. We had great days and some tough times, but we were all in it together. I realise I'm so lucky to have lined out with some of the greatest to ever do it in our game.

To all the managers I played under, with club and county, especially my uncle Páidí, Jack O'Connor, Pat O'Shea and Éamonn Fitzmaurice.

To all my physios and doctors who got me on the pitch through the years, with a special mention to Dr Michael Finnerty, a proud Galwegian but one we'd nearly call a Kerryman at this stage, as well as Dr Dave Geaney and Ger Keane, who helped me feel a lot better when I hopped off his physio table compared to when I climbed on.

To Charlie Neligan who gave me my start with Kerry minors and all the county board chairmen secretaries, in particular Seán Walsh, Jerome Conway and Patrick 'The Bag' O'Sullivan.

Thanks to Listry GAA club and Listowel Emmets GAA club for giving me the opportunity to coach them and gain experience on the line. It's been a pleasure.

Thanks to Colm Stafford in GAA+ and all his staff, I've really enjoyed my time since I've retired working with first, GAAGo and now GAA+. To Trevor Twamley of Sports Endorse and their team, for his great advice and help over the last few years.

To Patrick O'Donoghue, Margaret Farrelly, Fiona Murphy, Iollann Ó Murchú and everyone at Gill Books who've worked so hard to bring this book to fruition.

I would like to extend my heartfelt thanks to Adrian Russell, who not only authored this book but made the entire process an absolute pleasure. His talent speaks through every page, but what truly stood out was how easy-going, collaborative, and gracious he was throughout. Working with Adrian was effortless – in the best possible way – and I'm grateful for the experience.

I came from a great family and was fortunate to find another. To my mother- and father-in-law, Marian and Tadhg McGillicuddy, for always having a warm welcome for me in their home ever since Ellen and I began seeing each other. And to all the extended McGillicuddy family.

I've relied on Tadhg, in particular, for his wise advice on whatever the topic may be – professional or sport – and he has always been a valued sounding board for me.

To our kids, Alice, Tadhg and Tommy, who give us so much enjoyment and happiness and who we are so proud of. Watching them growing up fills us both with joy.

And finally, to Ellen, who I'd be lost without. Through the tough times and the great times, she's always there, always minding me and making sure I do the right thing. Like the one I came from, she has created a happy, welcoming home.

She could not make me happier. Thanks Ellen, I love you. Here's to the next chapter.

Dún Chaoin
km
12
R559
An Daingean
MORIARTY'S
FARMHOUSE
ALL ROOMS